# PASTA BY DESIGN

# PASTA BY DESIGN

George L. Legendre

Foreword by **Paola Antonelli**
Photography by **Stefano Graziani**
Based on an idea by **Marco Guarnieri**

189 illustrations, 93 in color

*For Antonia and Ioli, with love*

**George L. Legendre** is a designer, essayist and principal of
the London-based architectural firm IJP, which explores the
intersection between space, mathematics and computation.
The practice has built Henderson Waves, a 1000-foot-long
bridge in Singapore designed with a single mathematical
equation, and was shortlisted for the PS1/MoMA Young
Architect Program pavilion in 2011. Legendre has taught at
the London Architectural Association, Princeton University
and Harvard's Graduate School of Design, and written *IJP:
The Book of Surfaces*, and *Bodyline: The End of our Meta-
Mechanical Body*. He works in London.

After training as an architect at IAUV Venice, **Stefano Graziani**
took up photography and began collaborating with many
international magazines. He is the author of several books,
notably *Taxonomies*, *L'isola* and *Under the Volcano and
Other Stories*.

On the cover, a *farfalla*, page 063
Pages 2–3, a *cavatappo*, page 039
Page 6, a *galletto*, page 086

Copyright © 2011 George L. Legendre
Foreword Copyright © 2011 Paola Antonelli
Photographs Copyright © 2011 Stefano Graziani

Text, Phylogenetic Chart and Equations by
   George L. Legendre and Jean-Aimé Shu for IJP
The Family Reunion illustration by
   Woonyin Mo Wong for IJP
Layouts by Niccolo Marini for KGA
Original book design by IJP

First published in 2011 in hardcover in the United States
of America by Thames & Hudson Inc., 500 Fifth Avenue,
New York, New York 10110

thamesandhudsonusa.com

Library of Congress Catalog Card Number 2011922626

ISBN 978-0-500-51580-8

Printed and bound in China by Toppan Printing

# CONTENTS

**007**  Finish Your Design, Darling! by Paola Antonelli

**008**  Capturing the Essence of Pasta by George L. Legendre

**010**  The Family Tree (Phylogenetic Diagram)

**013**  The Architecture of Pasta: A User's Guide

**014**  Pasta from *acini* to *ziti*

*acini di pepe / agnolotti / anellini / bucatini / buccoli / calamaretti / cannelloni / cannolicchi rigati / capellini / cappelletti / casarecce / castellane / cavatappi / cavatelli / chifferi rigati / colonne Pompeii / conchiglie rigate / conchigliette lisce / conchiglioni rigati / corallini lisci / creste di galli / cuoretti / ditali rigati / fagottini / farfalle / farfalline / farfalloni / festonati / fettuccine / fiocchi rigati / fisarmoniche / funghini / fusilli / fusilli al ferretto / fusilli Capri / fusilli lunghi bucati / galletti / garganelli / gemelli / gigli / giglio ondulato / gnocchetti sardi / gnocchi / gramigna / lancette / lasagna larga doppia riccia / linguine / lumaconi rigati / maccheroni / maccheroni alla chitarra / mafaldine / manicotti / orecchiette / paccheri / pappardelle / penne rigate / pennoni lisci / pennoni rigati / puntalette / quadrefiore / quadretti / racchette / radiatori / ravioli quadrati / ravioli tondi / riccioli / riccioli ai cinque sapori / rigatoni / rombi / rotelle / saccottini / sagnarelli / sagne incannulate / scialatielli / spaccatelle / spaghetti / spirali / stellette / stortini / strozzapreti / tagliatelle / taglierini / tagliolini / torchietti / tortellini / tortiglioni / trenne / tripoline / trofie / trottole / tubetti rigati / ziti*

**198**  The Family Reunion (Seating Plan)

**206**  Index of Commonly Known Pasta Types

**208**  Acknowledgments

# FINISH YOUR DESIGN, DARLING!

Pasta, that simple and yet surprisingly versatile mixture of durum wheat-flour and water, shaped by hand or machine, is a delicious example of great design. Just like any other indispensable invention, pasta matches the available resources (wheat – one of the most widely produced cereals in the world) with goals (the human need not only to eat, but also to have a somewhat diversified diet). As well as being a design born out of necessity, it is also such a simple and strong concept that it has generated an almost endless variety of derivative pasta types – and an even greater number of dishes made from them. Moreover, it has proven to be a timeless design; although pasta's production tools may have been updated across the centuries, its basic forms have remained the same. It is also a global design, easy to appropriate and adapt to local culture – as can be seen from the many regional varieties of pasta dishes across the world. Finally, pasta is a universal success with both critics and the public, thus also passing the market-driven design test.

Considering the hundreds of different types of pasta that can be obtained, the manufacturing process is relatively simple and consistent. The dough is extruded and cut, or thinned and cut, and sometimes further manipulated – for instance, curled or pinched. These straightforward processes provide pasta with different characteristics, some of which can be objectively described, while others are so subtle only palates can detect them. The first, simpler, classification of pasta is in respect of their length: varieties exist that are long, short or, for soups, extra short. A second classification relates to the sauce that will be used. There are many empirical methods of classifying pasta, but ultimately each shape has its own unique character – some pasta recipe books look more like design instruction manuals than simple collections of cooking suggestion.

As a design buff, I have been working for a long time on my own way to read and classify pasta according to design criteria, manufacturing methods and material culture sources, but of all the pasta taxonomies ever conceived, George L. Legendre's is certainly one of the most original and poetic. In our contemporary world, where scientists like to flaunt their imperfection and vulnerability, programmers talk about the beauty of code, and architects and designers tinker with algorithms and software to achieve organic formal and structural behaviours, seeing mathematics in *fusilli* makes perfect sense. Although Sora Nina (that perfect chef next door) may well cook up a *cappelletti* with a standard deviation to give Legendre nightmares....

Paola Antonelli

# CAPTURING THE ESSENCE OF PASTA

The architect Marco Guarnieri and I share a professional address in a quiet lane off Bermondsey Street in south London. On most evenings we mill about the office's communal table and share our impressions of the day's crop of practical problems, delayed professional fees, contractual instructions and interim certificates. But first we sit down and eat pasta.

Being Italian, Marco knows all about it. It takes him around eight minutes to prepare the simplest of *pastasciuttas*, a dish of *spaghetti all'aglio, olio e peperoncino*. He usually starts by bringing six quarts of salted water to the boil, adds some *spaghetti* and lets it cook for about six to eight minutes until al dente. Next he drains the pasta in a colander, taking care not to rinse it with water so it does not loose its starch, and heats some olive oil in a skillet. When the oil begins to smoke, he stirs in two evenly chopped cloves of garlic and fries them over a medium-high heat until fragrant. He adds some red-pepper flakes and stirs it for another minute, before tossing the pasta into the pan. He mixes it energetically, and dinner is served. Sadly it takes us no more than a few minutes to finish our portions. Still hungry at first, staring at plates smeared with browned garlic and burnt olive oil, we feel vaguely disappointed. Then starch starts easing its way into our stomachs and the nagging discomfort turns into a state of mellowness, no doubt helped by large amounts of

Chianti. During one of these evenings, the concept for this book emerged.

Its concept is simple: to figure out the mathematical formulas of pasta and use the results to produce an inventory, guide and culinary resource that is both beautiful and useful. With over two hundred elaborate diagrams and photographs, as well as a few words on regional provenance and cuisine, *Pasta by Design* offers a surreal interpretation of the everyday experience of making and eating pasta. Specifically, it presents a magnified view of the *forming* stage of the pasta-making process (the mechanical extrusion of a mixture of durum wheat-flour and water into the familiar shape). Drawing on several years of practical experience – my architectural firm IJP has been using mathematics to design anything from pedestrian bridges to playground slides for a number of years – we have used mathematics to model reality and make it fun.

There is a huge canon of pasta, and often names or forms overlap, or become confused. Many regions in Italy produce lesser-known varieties of pasta, or spawn minor variations of established ones, then give them local names. This all makes classification a particularly difficult task, requiring the sort of knowledge of custom and tradition that ethnographers or anthropologists possess. This book takes on the challenge of classifying these pasta types in its own unique way. Freely inspired by the science of phylogeny (the study of relatedness among groups of natural forms), *Pasta by Design* pares down the startling variety of pasta to ninety-two unique types, divided according to their morphological features, and charts them in the Family Tree (pages 010–011). Each member of the family is then illustrated by its parametric equations, a 3D diagram and a specially commissioned photograph by Stefano Graziani. Combined, these representations capture the essence of each pasta, and give a concise, elegant and unique expression of a familiar thing. The book concludes with the Family Reunion, a reshuffle of the Family Tree into a 'bubble diagram' (a seating plan-cum-map) in which various relatives of the extended pasta family are hoarded together by similarities in shape and feature. A comprehensive index of commonly known pasta concludes the volume.

This quirky but serious publication was produced for anyone wishing to treat their significant other to something unusual, or those who, like the author, love their food but do not cook as often as they should. Foodies will appreciate it as a resource of pasta shapes and preparation tips; students of architecture and graphic design will be inspired by the diagrams and photographs of complex forms; and, lastly, the virtuosity of the equation-writing will intrigue anyone with an interest in mathematics or science.

The world of mathematics, with its complexity and arcane symbols, can be forbidding at the best of times – but not so with this book. In the course of planning it, we encountered time and again the warmest of reactions. On receiving a sample page of the unsolicited typescript, our (future) editor at Thames & Hudson saluted, enthusiastically, our 'insanity'. A prominent structural engineer, inspired by the sight of pasta shapes lying around our office, sighed and wished he too had more time to 'have fun'. A high school student on the lookout for a placement had his headmaster call us about the 'job with the pasta' (he sounded unsure). In a coffee shop near central London, a stranger with impeccable manners interrupted our conversation to enquire about the proofs on the table. And, finally, during an international mathematics conference, the distinguished historian of science Amy Dahan leaned towards me to enquire what Jean-Aimé Shu (the IJP project associate with whom I co-produced this book) was 'going on about' at the lectern. I could see why she sought clarification: Jean-Aimé's talk on topological invariants was broadcast on a video screen filled, by way of a surreal disclaimer, with a nine-foot-tall photograph of a golden *saccotino* (see page 155). She seemed genuinely intrigued.

George L. Legendre

# THE FAMILY TREE
## (Phylogenetic Diagram)

| | EDGES | SURFACE | CROSS-SECTION | LONGITUDINAL PROFILE |
|---|---|---|---|---|
| | SMOOTH | SMOOTH | SOLID | TWISTED |
| | CRENELLATED | STRIATED | HOLLOW | HELICOIDAL |
| | | | SEMI-OPEN | PINCHED |
| | | | | BUNCHED |

DIMENSIONS

Ø  W  L  (mm)

| Ø | W | L | name | code | EDGES | SURFACE | CROSS-SECTION | LONGITUDINAL PROFILE |
|---|---|---|---|---|---|---|---|---|
| - | 20 | 300 | colonne Pompeii | | | | | |
| - | 8 | 100 | fusilli al ferretto | | | | | |
| - | 16 | 170 | fusilli Capri | | | | | |
| - | 10 | 33 | fusilli | TW_SO_SM_SM | SMOOTH | SMOOTH | SOLID | |
| - | 6 | 38 | gemelli | | | | | |
| - | 4 | 50 | trofie | | | | | |
| 3 | 27 | 210 | fusilli lunghi bucati | TW_HO_SM_SM | SMOOTH | SMOOTH | HOLLOW | TWISTED |
| - | 7 | 43 | casarecce | | | | | |
| - | 7 | 53 | strozzapreti | TW_SE_SM_SM | SMOOTH | SMOOTH | SEMI-OPEN | |
| 27 | - | 250 | sagne incannulate | | | | | |
| 8 | - | 30 | buccoli | | | | | |
| 20 | - | - | cappelletti | HE_HO_SM_SM | SMOOTH | | | |
| - | 10 | 29 | gigli | | | | | |
| 15 | - | 28 | trottole | | | SMOOTH | | |
| | | | | | CRENELLATED | | | |
| - | 15 | 30 | giglio ondulato | HE_HO_SM_CR | | | HOLLOW | HELICOIDAL |
| 6 | 13 | 36 | cavatappi | | | | | |
| - | 15 | 33 | spirali | HE_HO_ST_SM | SMOOTH | STRIATED | | |
| - | 5 | 15 | lancette | | | | | |
| - | 3 | 9 | puntalette | PI_SO_SM_SM | SMOOTH | | | |
| - | 30 | 41 | farfalle | | | SMOOTH | | |
| - | 7 | 14 | farfalline | | | | | |
| - | 34 | 50 | farfalloni | PI_SO_SM_CR | CRENELLATED | | | |
| - | 7 | 8 | funghini | | | | | |
| - | 23 | 33 | fiocchi rigati | PI_SO_ST_SM | SMOOTH | STRIATED | SOLID | _LEFT |
| - | 30 | 30 | fagottini | | | | | |
| - | 20 | 30 | saccottini | PI_HO_SM_SM | SMOOTH | | | |
| - | 16 | 20 | tortellini | | | SMOOTH | | |
| - | 30 | 45 | agnolotti | | | | HOLLOW | PINCHED |
| - | 50 | 50 | ravioli quadrati | PI_HO_SM_CR | CRENELLATED | | | |
| - | 50 | 50 | ravioli tondi | | | | | |
| - | 7 | 12 | conchigliette lisce | PI_SE_SM_SM | SMOOTH | SMOOTH | | |
| - | 13 | 35 | castellane | | | | | |
| - | 23 | 37 | conchiglie rigate | | | | SEMI-OPEN | |
| - | 36 | 65 | conchiglioni rigati | | | | | |
| - | 7 | 22 | gnocchetti sardi | | | | | |
| - | 16 | 32 | gnocchi | PI_SE_ST_SM | SMOOTH | STRIATED | | |
| - | 15 | 35 | riccioli | BU_SE_SM_SM | SMOOTH | | | |
| - | 16 | 23 | fisarmoniche | | | SMOOTH | SEMI-OPEN | BUNCHED |
| - | 17 | 24 | radiatori | BU_SE_SM_CR | CRENELLATED | | | |

STRAIGHT      SOLID           SMOOTH     SMOOTH
SHEARED       HOLLOW          STRIATED   CRENELLATED
BENT          SEMI-OPEN

| name | Ø | W | L |
|---|---|---|---|
| acini di pepe | 2 | – | 3 |
| capellini | 1 | – | 260 |
| cuoretti | – | 3 | 4 |
| linguine | – | 3 | 255 |
| quadretti | – | 6 | 6 |
| scialatielli | – | 10 | 100 |
| spaghetti | 2 | – | 255 |
| stortini | – | 3 | 10 |
| maccheroni alla chitarra | | | |
| lasagna larga doppia riccia | – | 75 | 170 |
| mafaldine | – | 13 | 240 |
| quadrefiore | 15 | – | 35 |
| sagnarelli | – | 20 | 55 |
| tropoline | – | 8 | 257 |
| ancllini | 6 | – | – |
| bucatini | 3 | – | 237 |
| calamaretti | 25 | – | 14 |
| cannelloni | 23 | – | 100 |
| corallini lisci | 3 | – | 4 |
| paccheri | – | 29 | 46 |
| racchette | – | 15 | 31 |
| stellette | – | 4 | 4 |
| ziti | 7 | – | 255 |
| cannolicchi rigati | 8 | – | 41 |
| ditali rigati | 8 | – | 9 |
| festonati | – | 15 | 46 |
| garganelli | – | 9 | 36 |
| maccheroni | 8 | – | 40 |
| manicotti | – | 35 | 130 |
| rigatoni | 16 | – | 40 |
| rotelle | 21 | – | – |
| tortiglioni | 10 | – | 45 |
| cavatelli | – | 12 | 28 |
| orecchiette | 20 | 7 | – |
| fettuccine | – | 7 | 150 |
| pappardelle | 50 | 18 | – |
| tagliatelle | 65 | 6 | – |
| taglierini | 70 | 2 | – |
| tagliolini | 60 | 1 | – |
| creste di galli | 8 | 20 | 36 |
| gramigna | 3 | 13 | 26 |
| chifferi rigati | 7 | 10 | 17 |
| galletti | 8 | 15 | 36 |
| lumaconi rigati | – | 38 | 47 |
| torchietti | – | 8 | 47 |
| tubetti rigati | 5 | – | 11 |
| riccioli ai cinque sapori | – | 8 | 36 |
| spaccatelle | – | 7 | 33 |
| rombi | – | 24 | 46 |
| pennoni lisci | – | 28 | 75 |
| trenne | – | 13 | 58 |
| penne rigate | 8 | – | 55 |
| pennoni rigati | – | 28 | 84 |

**_RIGHT**

STRAIGHT
  SOLID
    SMOOTH
      SMOOTH — ST_SO_SM_SM
      CRENELLATED — ST_SO_SM_CR
  HOLLOW
    SMOOTH
      SMOOTH — ST_HO_SM_SM
    STRIATED
      SMOOTH — ST_HO_ST_SM
  SEMI-OPEN
    SMOOTH
      SMOOTH — ST_SE_SM_SM
    STRIATED
      CRENELLATED — ST_SE_ST_CR

BENT
  SOLID
    SMOOTH
      SMOOTH — BE_SO_SM_SM
  HOLLOW
    SMOOTH
      SMOOTH — BE_HO_SM_SM
    STRIATED
      SMOOTH — BE_HO_ST_SM
  SEMI-OPEN
    SMOOTH
      SMOOTH — BE_SE_SM_SM

SHEARED
  SOLID
    SMOOTH
      CRENELLATED — SH_SO_SM_CR
  HOLLOW
    SMOOTH
      SMOOTH — SH_HO_SM_SM
    STRIATED
      SMOOTH — SH_HO_ST_SM

DRYING

PACKING

# THE ARCHITECTURE OF PASTA: A USER'S GUIDE

A speciality of the northern Italian region of Emilia-Romagna, *gramigna* (little weed) are traditionally served with a chunky sauce of sausages, or accompanied by the world-famous *ragù alla bolognese*. Alternatively, *gramigna* are sometimes presented *alla pomodoro* (with a light tomato sauce).

> BENT LONGITUDINAL PROFILE

⌄ HOLLOW CROSS-SECTION

⌄ SMOOTH SURFACE

⌄ SMOOTH EDGES

_ranges

$i := 0, 1 .. \; 25$

$j := 0, 1 .. \; 150$

A range is a series of numbers used in the equations. There are two ranges, arbitrarily named *i* and *j*. Ranges vary between 0 and 1 – or any multiple thereof.

A brief text explaining the etymological and historical derivation of the pasta, as well as giving example dishes. Unless otherwise stated, ingredients are durum wheat-flour and water.

_equations

$$\Pi_{i,j} := \left[ 0.5 + 5.6 \cdot \left( \frac{j}{150} \right)^2 + 0.3 \cdot \cos \left( \frac{2 \cdot i}{25} \cdot \pi \right) \right] \cdot \cos \left( \frac{2.1 \cdot j}{150} \cdot \pi \right)$$

$$\Theta_{i,j} := 0.3 \cdot \sin \left( \frac{2 \cdot i}{25} \cdot \pi \right)$$

$$K_{i,j} := \left[ 0.5 + 3.2 \left( \frac{j}{150} \right)^2 + 0.3 \cdot \cos \left( \frac{2 \cdot i}{25} \cdot \pi \right) \right] \cdot \sin \left( \frac{2.1 \cdot j}{150} \cdot \pi \right)$$

Find out where *gramigna* is located in our Pasta Family Tree – and why (page 010).

Named after $(\Pi, \Theta, K)$, three letters from the Greek alphabet, these three equations form the 'genetic code' of the pasta shape. Because the shape is 3D, we need three equations to represent it. Each equation sets the measurements in a separate dimension: width, length and depth. These equations feature simple mathematical functions that use the ranges defined above to 'plot' the form.

*Gramigna* in 3D. Each dot combines the solutions of all three equations shown above for a given value of ranges *i* and *j*. The numbers on the axes are not measurements, but values of the solutions of each equation (the form is not 'plotted' to scale).

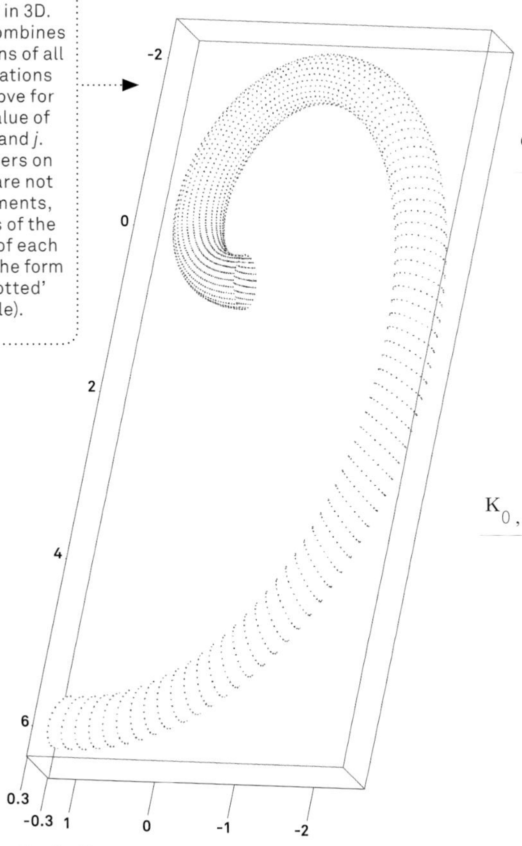

$(\Pi, \Theta, K)$

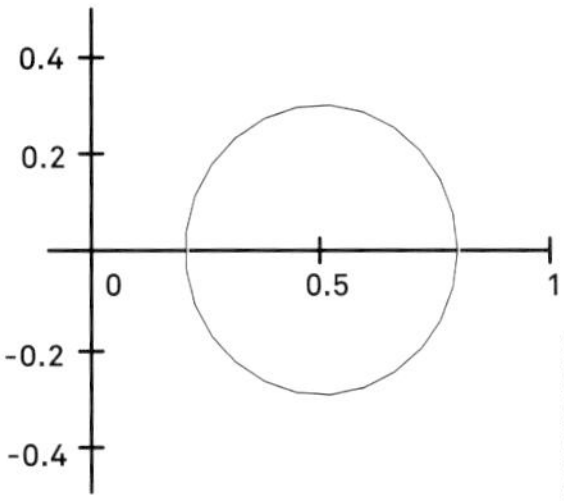

$\Theta_{i,0}$

$\Pi_{i,1}$

Solving equations Θ and Π for j=0, j=1, and i=0 to 25 gives us the circular cross-section of *gramigna*. We used this and other, similar results to place the shape in the Pasta Family Tree.

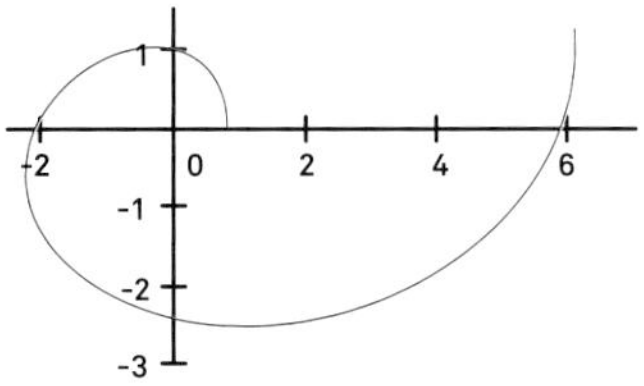

$K_{0,j}$

$\Pi_{0,j}$

Check the absolute cooking time and average dimensions of those *graminga* surveyed. (Cooking times may vary, so consult manufacturer's instructions.)

Length: 26 mm | Width: 13 mm
Diameter: 3 mm
Cooking time: 9 min

# ACINI DI PEPE

The smallest member of the *pastine minute* (tiny pasta) family, *acini di pepe* (peppercorns) are most suited to consommés (clear soups), with the occasional addition of croutons and diced greens. Made of durum-wheat flour and eggs, *acini di pepe* are commonly used in the Italian-American 'wedding soup', a broth of vegetables and meat.

> STRAIGHT LONGITUDINAL PROFILE
ˇ SOLID CROSS-SECTION
ˇ SMOOTH SURFACE
ˇ SMOOTH EDGES

_ranges

$i := 0, 1 .. 120$

$j := 0, 1 .. 30$

_equations

$$\Pi_{i,j} := 15 \cdot \cos\left(\frac{i}{60} \cdot \pi\right)$$

$$\Theta_{i,j} := 15 \cdot \sin\left(\frac{i}{60} \cdot \pi\right)$$

$$K_{i,j} := j$$

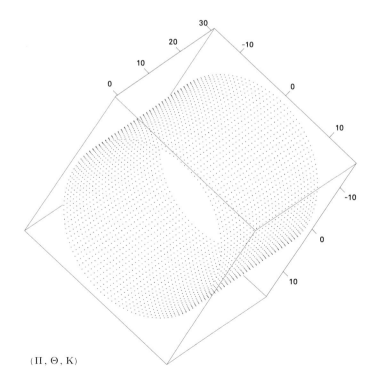

$(\Pi, \Theta, K)$

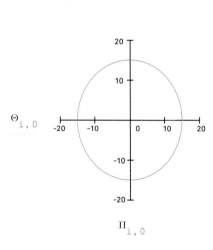

$\Theta_{i,0}$

$\Pi_{i,0}$

Length: 3 mm | Diameter: 2 mm
Cooking Time: 9 min

# AGNOLOTTI

These shell-like *ravioli* from Piedmont, northern Italy, are fashioned from small pieces of flattened dough made of wheat flour and egg, and are often filled with braised veal, pork, vegetables or cheese. The true *agnolotto* should feature a crinkled edge, cut using a fluted pasta wheel. Recommended with melted butter and sage.

> PINCHED LONGITUDINAL PROFILE
ᵛ HOLLOW CROSS-SECTION
ᵛ SMOOTH SURFACE
ᵛ CRENELLATED EDGES

_ranges

$i := 0, 1 .. \ 60$

$j := 0, 1 .. \ 100$

_equations

$$\Pi_{i,j} := \left(10 \cdot \sin\left(\frac{i}{120} \cdot \pi\right)^{0.5} + \frac{i}{400} \cdot \sin\left(\frac{3 \cdot j}{10} \cdot \pi\right)\right) \cdot \cos\left(\frac{19 \cdot j}{2000} \cdot \pi + 0.03 \cdot \pi\right)$$

$$\Theta_{i,j} := \left(10 \cdot \sin\left(\frac{i}{120} \cdot \pi\right) + \frac{i}{400} \cdot \cos\left(\frac{3 \cdot j}{10} \cdot \pi\right)\right) \cdot \sin\left(\frac{19 \cdot j}{2000} \cdot \pi + 0.03 \cdot \pi\right)$$

$$K_{i,j} := 5 \cdot \cos\left(\frac{i}{120} \cdot \pi\right)^{5} \cdot \sin\left(\frac{j}{100} \cdot \pi\right) - 5 \cdot \sin\left(\frac{j}{100} \cdot \pi\right) \cdot \cos\left(\frac{i}{120} \cdot \pi\right)^{200}$$

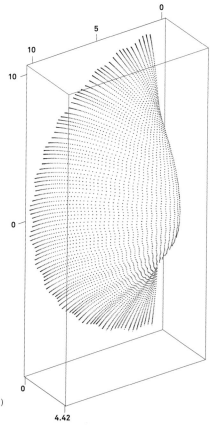

$(\Pi, \Theta, K)$

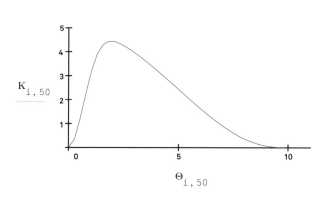

$\dfrac{K_{i,50}}{}$

$\Theta_{i,50}$

Length: 45 mm | Width: 30 mm
Cooking Time: 10 min

# ANELLINI

The diminutive *anellini* (small rings) are part of the extended *pastine minute* (tiny pasta) clan. Their thickness varies between only 1.15 and 1.20 mm, and they are therefore usually found in light soups together with croutons and thinly sliced vegetables. This pasta may also be found served in a *timballo* (baked pasta dish).

> STRAIGHT LONGITUDINAL PROFILE

∨ HOLLOW CROSS-SECTION

∨ SMOOTH SURFACE

∨ SMOOTH EDGES

_ranges

$i := 0, 1 .. \ 200$

$j := 0, 1 .. \ 8$

_equations

$$\Pi_{i,j} := \cos(0.01 \cdot i \cdot \pi)$$

$$\Theta_{i,j} := 1.1 \cdot \sin(0.01 \cdot i \cdot \pi)$$

$$K_{i,j} := 0.05 \cdot j$$

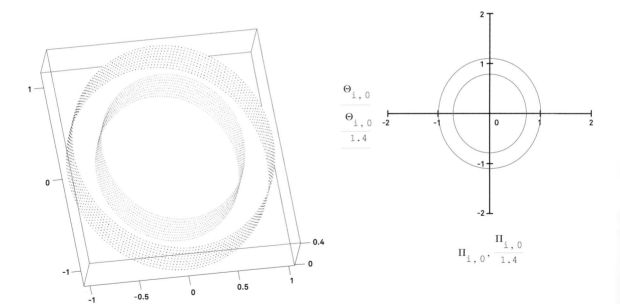

$$(\Pi, \Theta, K), \left(\frac{\Pi}{1.4}, \frac{\Theta}{1.4}, K\right)$$

$$\Theta_{i,0}$$

$$\frac{\Theta_{i,0}}{1.4}$$

$$\Pi_{i,0}, \frac{\Pi_{i,0}}{1.4}$$

Diameter: 6 mm | Thickness: 1 mm
Cooking Time: 6 min

# BUCATINI

*Bucatini* (pierced) pasta is commonly served as a *pastasciutta* (pasta boiled, drained and dished up with a sauce, rather than in broth). Its best-known accompaniment is *amatriciana*: a hearty traditional sauce made with dried pork, Pecorino Romano and tomato sauce, and named after the medieval town of Amatrice in central Italy.

> STRAIGHT LONGITUDINAL PROFILE
  ∨ HOLLOW CROSS-SECTION
    ∨ SMOOTH SURFACE
      ∨ SMOOTH EDGES

_ranges

$i := 0, 1 .. 60$

$j := 0, 1 .. 90$

_equations

$$\Pi_{i,j} := 0.3 \cdot \cos\left(\frac{i}{30} \cdot \pi\right)$$

$$\Theta_{i,j} := 0.3 \cdot \sin\left(\frac{i}{30} \cdot \pi\right)$$

$$K_{i,j} := \frac{j}{45}$$

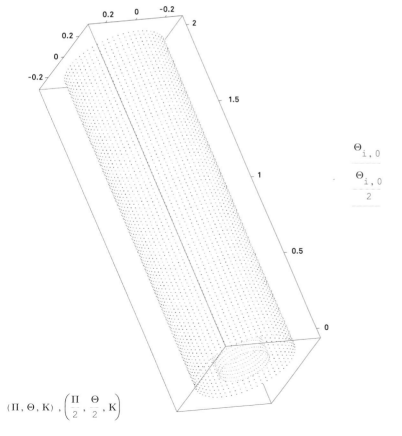

$$(\Pi, \Theta, K) , \left(\frac{\Pi}{2}, \frac{\Theta}{2}, K\right)$$

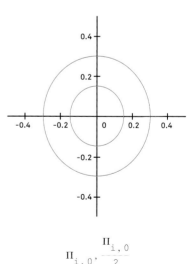

$$\Theta_{i,0}$$
$$\frac{\Theta_{i,0}}{2}$$

$$\Pi_{i,0}, \frac{\Pi_{i,0}}{2}$$

Length: 237 mm | Diameter: 3 mm
Cooking Time: 11 min

# BUCCOLI

A spiral-shaped example from the *pasta corta* (short pasta) family, and of rather uncertain pedigree, *buccoli* are suitable in a mushroom and sausage dish. They are also excellent with a tomato, aubergine, pesto and ricotta salad.

> HELICOIDAL LONGITUDINAL PROFILE
⌄ HOLLOW CROSS-SECTION
⌄ SMOOTH SURFACE
⌄ SMOOTH EDGES

_ranges

$i := 0, 1 .. \ 200$

$j := 0, 1 .. \ 25$

_equations

$$\Pi_{i,j} := \left( 0.7 + 0.2 \cdot \sin\left( \frac{21 \cdot j}{250} \cdot \pi \right) \right) \cdot \cos\left( \frac{i}{20} \cdot \pi \right)$$

$$\Theta_{i,j} := \left( 0.7 + 0.2 \cdot \sin\left( \frac{21 \cdot j}{250} \cdot \pi \right) \right) \cdot \sin\left( \frac{-i}{20} \cdot \pi \right)$$

$$K_{i,j} := \frac{39 \cdot i}{1000} + 1.5 \cdot \sin\left( \frac{j}{50} \cdot \pi \right)$$

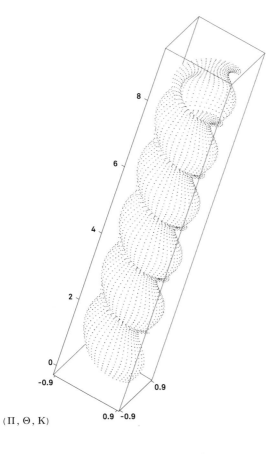

$(\Pi, \Theta, K)$

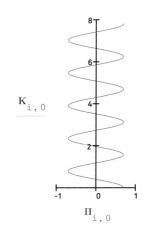

$K_{i,0}$

$\Pi_{i,0}$

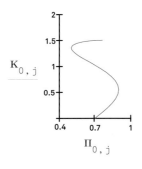

$K_{0,j}$

$\Pi_{0,j}$

Length: 30 mm | Diameter: 8 mm
Cooking Time: 8 min

# CALAMARETTI

Literally 'little squids', *calamaretti* are small ring-shaped pasta cooked as *pastasciutta* (pasta boiled and drained) then dished up with a tomato-, egg- or cheese-based sauce. Their shape means that *calamaretti* hold both chunky and thin sauces equally well. Fittingly, they are often served with seafood.

> STRAIGHT LONGITUDINAL PROFILE
ⱽ HOLLOW CROSS-SECTION
ⱽ SMOOTH SURFACE
ⱽ SMOOTH EDGES

_ranges

$i := 0, 1 .. 150$

$j := 0, 1 .. 20$

_equations

$$\Pi_{i,j} := \cos\left(\frac{i}{75} \cdot \pi\right) + 0.1 \cdot \cos\left(\frac{j}{40} \cdot \pi\right) + 0.1 \cdot \cos\left(\frac{i}{75} \cdot \pi + \frac{j}{40} \cdot \pi\right)$$

$$\Theta_{i,j} := 1.2 \cdot \sin\left(\frac{i}{75} \cdot \pi\right) + 0.2 \cdot \sin\left(\frac{j}{40} \cdot \pi\right)$$

$$K_{i,j} := \frac{j}{10}$$

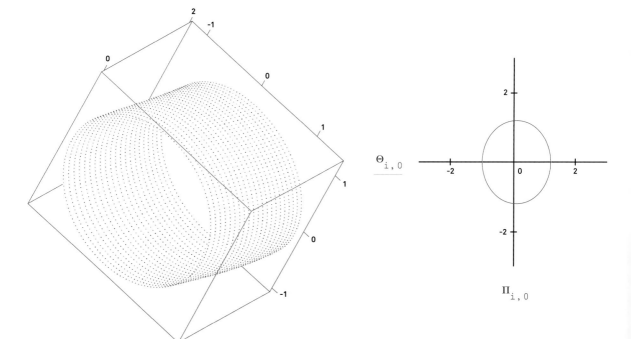

$(\Pi, \Theta, K)$

$\Theta_{i,0}$

$\Pi_{i,0}$

Length: 14 mm | Diameter: 25 mm
Cooking Time: 14 min

# CANNELLONI

Made with wheat flour, eggs and olive oil, *cannelloni* (big tubes) originate as strips of pasta shaped into perfect cylinders, which can be stuffed with meat, vegetables or ricotta. The stuffed *cannelloni* are covered with a creamy *besciamella* sauce, a sprinkling of Parmigiano-Reggiano cheese and then oven-baked.

> STRAIGHT LONGITUDINAL PROFILE
>> ⌄ HOLLOW CROSS-SECTION
>>> ⌄ SMOOTH SURFACE
>>>> ⌄ SMOOTH EDGES

_ranges

$i := 0, 1 .. 110$

$j := 0, 1 .. 50$

_equations

$$\Pi_{i,j} := \left(1 + \frac{j}{100}\right) \cdot \cos\left(\frac{i}{55} \cdot \pi\right) + 0.5 \cdot \cos\left(\frac{j}{100} \cdot \pi\right) + 0.1 \cdot \cos\left(\frac{i}{55} \cdot \pi + \frac{j}{125} \cdot \pi\right)$$

$$\Theta_{i,j} := 1.3 \cdot \sin\left(\frac{i}{55} \cdot \pi\right) + 0.3 \cdot \sin\left(\frac{j}{100} \cdot \pi\right)$$

$$K_{i,j} := \frac{7 \cdot j}{50}$$

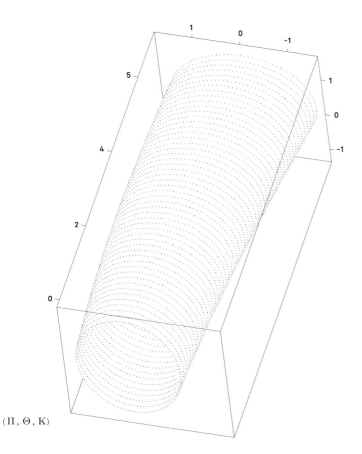

$(\Pi, \Theta, K)$

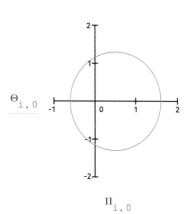

$\Theta_{i,0}$

$\Pi_{i,0}$

Length: **100 mm** | Diameter: **23 mm**
Cooking Time: **20 min**

# CANNOLICCHI RIGATI

Known as 'little tubes', *cannolicchi* exist both in a *rigati* (grooved) and *lisci* (smooth) form. These hollow *pasta corta* (short pasta) come in various diameters and are often served with seafood. *Cannolicchi* hail from Campania in southern Italy.

> STRAIGHT LONGITUDINAL PROFILE
> ⌄ HOLLOW CROSS-SECTION
> ⌄ STRIATED SURFACE
> ⌄ SMOOTH EDGES

_ranges

$i := 0, 1 .. 140$

$j := 0, 1 .. 50$

_equations

$$\Pi_{i,j} := 8 \cdot \cos\left(\frac{i}{70} \cdot \pi\right) + 0.2 \cdot \cos\left(\frac{2 \cdot i}{7} \cdot \pi\right) + 5 \cdot \cos\left(\frac{j}{100} \cdot \pi\right)$$

$$\Theta_{i,j} := 8 \cdot \sin\left(\frac{i}{70} \cdot \pi\right) + 0.2 \cdot \sin\left(\frac{2 \cdot i}{7} \cdot \pi\right) + 4 \cdot \sin\left(\frac{j}{100} \cdot \pi\right)$$

$$K_{i,j} := \frac{6 \cdot j}{5}$$

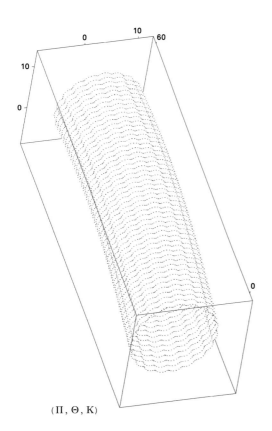

$(\Pi, \Theta, K)$

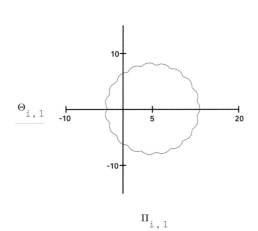

$\Theta_{i,1}$

$\Pi_{i,1}$

Length: 41 mm | Diameter: 8 mm
Cooking Time: 11 min

# CAPELLINI

An extra-fine rod-like pasta, *capellini* (thin hair) may be served in a light broth, but also combine perfectly with butter, nutmeg or lemon. This variety (or its even more slender relative, *capelli d'angelo*: 'angel hair') is sometimes used to form the basis of an unusual sweet pasta dish, made with lemons and almonds, called *torta ricciolina*.

> STRAIGHT LONGITUDINAL PROFILE
∨ SOLID CROSS-SECTION
∨ SMOOTH SURFACE
∨ SMOOTH EDGES

_ranges

$i := 0, 1 .. \ 15$

$j := 0, 1 .. \ 100$

_equations

$$\Pi_{i,j} := 0.05 \cdot \cos\left(\frac{2 \cdot i}{15} \cdot \pi\right) + 0.6 \cdot \cos\left(\frac{j}{100} \cdot \pi\right)$$

$$\Theta_{i,j} := 0.05 \cdot \sin\left(\frac{2 \cdot i}{15} \cdot \pi\right) + 0.5 \cdot \sin\left(\frac{j}{100} \cdot \pi\right)$$

$$K_{i,j} := \frac{7 \cdot j}{100}$$

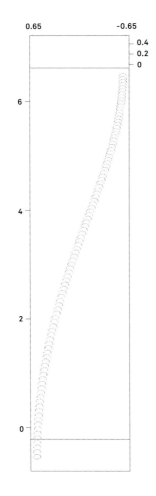

$(\Pi, \Theta, K)$

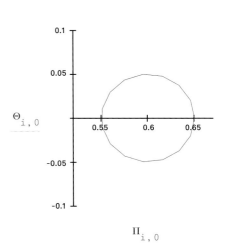

$\Theta_{i,0}$

$\Pi_{i,0}$

Length: 260 mm | Diameter: 1 mm
Cooking Time: 2 min

# CAPPELLETTI

This pasta is customarily served as the first course of a traditional north Italian Christmas meal, dished up in a chicken *brodo* (broth). Typically, it is the children of a household who prepare the *cappelletti* (little hats) on Christmas Eve, filling the pasta parcels (made from wheat flour and fresh eggs) with mixed meats or soft cheeses, such as ricotta.

> HELICOIDAL LONGITUDINAL PROFILE
⌄ HOLLOW CROSS-SECTION
⌄ SMOOTH SURFACE
⌄ SMOOTH EDGES

_ranges

$i := 0, 1 .. \ 40$

$j := 0, 1 .. \ 120$

_equations

$$\Pi_{i,j} := \left(0.1 + \sin\left(\frac{3 \cdot i}{160} \cdot \pi\right)\right) \cdot \cos\left(\frac{2.3 \cdot j}{120} \cdot \pi\right)$$

$$\Theta_{i,j} := \left(0.1 + \sin\left(\frac{3 \cdot i}{160} \cdot \pi\right)\right) \cdot \sin\left(\frac{2.3 \cdot j}{120} \cdot \pi\right)$$

$$K_{i,j} := 0.1 + \frac{j}{400} + \left(0.3 - 0.231 \cdot \frac{i}{40}\right) \cdot \cos\left(\frac{i}{20} \cdot \pi\right)$$

$K_{0,j}$

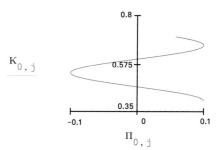

$\Pi_{0,j}$

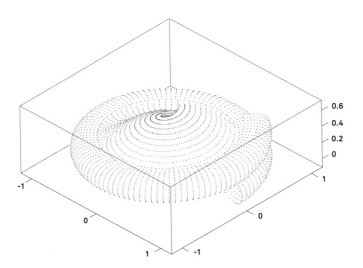

$(\Pi, \Theta, K)$

$K_{i,0}$

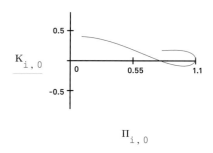

$\Pi_{i,0}$

Diameter: 20 mm | Thickness: 9 mm
Cooking Time: 9 min

# CASARECCE

Easily identified by their unique s-shaped cross-section, *casarecce* (home-made) are best cooked as *pastasciutta* (pasta boiled, drained and dished up with a sauce). Often *casarecce* are served with a classic *ragù* and topped with a sprinkle of pepper and Parmigiano-Reggiano cheese.

> TWISTED LONGITUDINAL PROFILE
>> SEMI-OPEN CROSS-SECTION
>> SMOOTH SURFACE
>> SMOOTH EDGES

_ranges

$i := 0, 1 .. \ 60$

$j := 0, 1 .. \ 60$

_equations

$$\Pi_{i,j} := if\left(i \leq 30, 0.5 \cdot \cos\left(\frac{j}{30} \cdot \pi\right) + 0.5 \cdot \cos\left(\frac{2 \cdot i + j + 16}{40} \cdot \pi\right), \cos\left(\frac{j}{40} \cdot \pi\right) + 0.5 \cdot \cos\left(\frac{j}{30} \cdot \pi\right) + 0.5 \cdot \sin\left(\frac{2 \cdot i - j}{40} \cdot \pi\right)\right)$$

$$\Theta_{i,j} := if\left(i \leq 30, 0.5 \cdot \sin\left(\frac{j}{30} \cdot \pi\right) + 0.5 \cdot \sin\left(\frac{2 \cdot i + j + 16}{40} \cdot \pi\right), \sin\left(\frac{j}{40} \cdot \pi\right) + 0.5 \cdot \sin\left(\frac{j}{30} \cdot \pi\right) + 0.5 \cdot \cos\left(\frac{2 \cdot i - j}{40} \cdot \pi\right)\right)$$

$$K_{i,j} := \frac{j}{4}$$

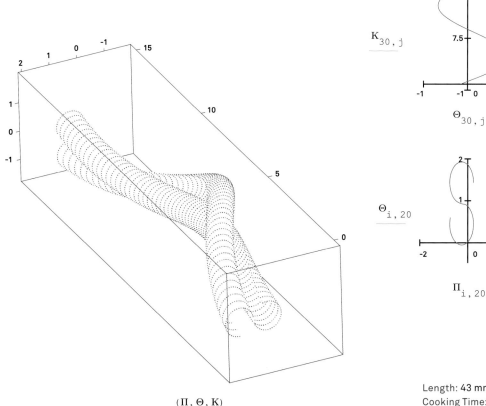

$K_{30,j}$

$\Theta_{30,j}$

$\Theta_{i,20}$

$\Pi_{i,20}$

$(\Pi, \Theta, K)$

Length: 43 mm | Width: 7 mm
Cooking Time: 11 min

# CASTELLANE

The manufacturer Barilla has recently created this elegant pasta shape. According to its maker, they were originally called *paguri* (hermit crabs) but renamed *castellane* (castle dwellers). The sturdy form and rich nutty taste of *castellane* stand up to hearty meats and full-flavoured sauces.

> PINCHED LONGITUDINAL PROFILE
> ⌄ SEMI-OPEN CROSS-SECTION
> ⌄ STRIATED SURFACE
> ⌄ SMOOTH EDGES

_ranges

$i := 0, 1 .. \ 60$

$j := 0, 1 .. \ 120$

_equations

$$\Pi_{i,j} := \left[ 0.3 \cdot \sin\left(\frac{j}{120} \cdot \pi\right) \cdot \left| \cos\left(\frac{j+3}{6} \cdot \pi\right) \right| + \frac{i^2}{720} \cdot \left( \sin\left(\frac{2 \cdot j}{300} \cdot \pi\right)^2 + 0.1 \right) + 0.3 \right] \cdot \cos\left(\frac{7 \cdot i}{150} \cdot \pi\right)$$

$$\Theta_{i,j} := \left[ 0.3 \cdot \sin\left(\frac{j}{120} \cdot \pi\right) \cdot \left| \cos\left(\frac{j+3}{6} \cdot \pi\right) \right| + \frac{i^2}{720} \cdot \left( \sin\left(\frac{2 \cdot j}{300} \cdot \pi\right)^2 + 0.1 \right) + 0.3 \right] \cdot \sin\left(\frac{7 \cdot i}{150} \cdot \pi\right)$$

$$K_{i,j} := 12 \cdot \cos\left(\frac{j}{120} \cdot \pi\right)$$

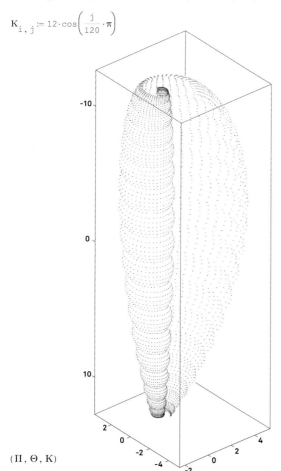

$(\Pi, \Theta, K)$

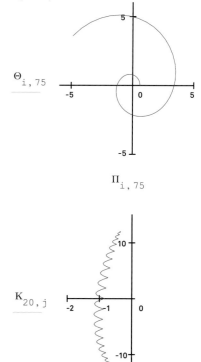

$\dfrac{\Theta_{i,75}}{\Pi_{i,75}}$

$\dfrac{K_{20,j}}{\Pi_{20,j}}$

Length: 35 mm | Width: 13 mm
Cooking Time: 9 min

# CAVATAPPI

Perfect with chunky sauces made from lamb or pork, *cavatappi* (corkscrews) are 36 mm-long, hollow helicoidal tubes. As well as an accompaniment to creamy sauces, such as *boscaiola* (woodsman's) sauce, they are also often used in oven-baked cheese-topped dishes, or in salads with pesto. (See the similar *spirali* on page 167.)

> HELICOIDAL LONGITUDINAL PROFILE
  ∨ HOLLOW CROSS-SECTION
    ∨ STRIATED SURFACE
      ∨ SMOOTH EDGES

_ranges

$i := 0, 1 .. \ 70$

$j := 0, 1 .. \ 150$

_equations

$$\Pi_{i,j} := \left(3 + 2 \cdot \cos\left(\frac{i}{35} \cdot \pi\right) + 0.1 \cdot \cos\left(\frac{2 \cdot i}{7} \cdot \pi\right)\right) \cdot \cos\left(\frac{j}{30} \cdot \pi\right)$$

$$\Theta_{i,j} := \left(3 + 2 \cdot \cos\left(\frac{i}{35} \cdot \pi\right) + 0.1 \cdot \cos\left(\frac{2 \cdot i}{7} \cdot \pi\right)\right) \cdot \sin\left(\frac{j}{30} \cdot \pi\right)$$

$$K_{i,j} := 3 + 2 \cdot \sin\left(\frac{i}{35} \cdot \pi\right) + 0.1 \cdot \sin\left(\frac{2 \cdot i}{7} \cdot \pi\right) + \frac{j}{6}$$

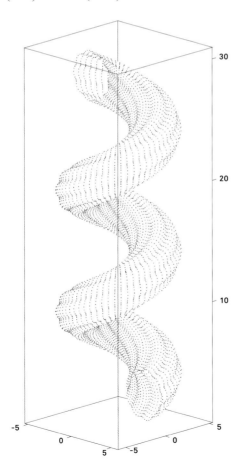

$(\Pi, \Theta, K)$

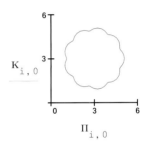

$K_{i,0}$

$\Pi_{i,0}$

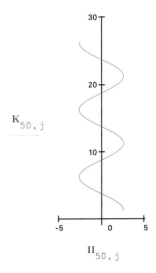

$K_{50,j}$

$\Pi_{50,j}$

Length: **36 mm** | Width: **13 mm**
Diameter: **6 mm**
Cooking Time: **11 min**

# CAVATELLI

Popular in the south of Italy, and related in shape to the longer twisted *casareccia* (see page 034), *cavatelli* can be served *alla puttanesca* (with a sauce containing chilli, garlic, capers and anchovies). They can also be added to a salad with olive oil, sautéed crushed garlic and a dusting of soft cheese.

(see page 034)

> STRAIGHT LONGITUDINAL PROFILE
> ⌄ SEMI-OPEN CROSS-SECTION
> ⌄ SMOOTH SURFACE
> ⌄ SMOOTH EDGES

_ranges

$i := 0, 1 .. 200$

$j := 0, 1 .. 30$

_equations

$$\alpha_i := 0.5 \cdot \cos\left(\frac{i}{100} \cdot \pi\right) \qquad \beta_{i,j} := \frac{j}{60} \cdot \sin\left(\frac{i}{100} \cdot \pi\right)$$

$$\Pi_{i,j} := 3\left(1 - \sin(\alpha_i \cdot 2\pi)\right) \cdot \cos(\alpha_i \cdot \pi + 0.9 \cdot \pi)$$

$$\Theta_{i,j} := 3\sin(\alpha_i \cdot 2\pi) \cdot \sin(\alpha_i \cdot \pi + 0.63 \cdot \pi)$$

$$K_{i,j} := 4 \cdot \beta_{i,j} \cdot \left(5 - \sin(\alpha_i \cdot \pi)\right)$$

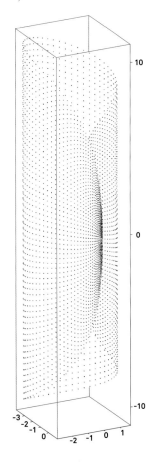

$(\Pi, \Theta, K)$

$\Theta_{i,10}$

$\Pi_{i,10}$

Length: 28 mm | Width: 12 mm
Thickness: 2 mm
Cooking Time: 14–16 min

# CHIFFERI RIGATI

This pasta – available in both *rigati* (grooved) and *lisci* (smooth) forms – is typically cooked in broth or served in *ragù alla bolognese*, though *chifferi rigati* also make an excellent addition to salads with carrot, red pepper and courgette. *Chifferi rigati* bear a resemblance to, and the term is a transliteration of, the Austrian 'kipfel' sweet.

> BENT LONGITUDINAL PROFILE
⌄ HOLLOW CROSS-SECTION
⌄ STRIATED SURFACE
⌄ SMOOTH EDGES

_ranges

$i := 0, 1 .. \ 200$

$j := 0, 1 .. \ 45$

_equations

$$\Pi_{i,j} := \left( 0.45 + 0.3 \cdot \cos\left(\frac{i}{100} \cdot \pi\right) + 0.005 \cdot \cos\left(\frac{2 \cdot i}{5} \cdot \pi\right)\right) \cdot \cos\left(\frac{j}{45} \cdot \pi\right) + 0.15 \cdot \left(\frac{j}{45}\right)^{10} \cdot \cos\left(\frac{i}{100} \cdot \pi\right)^3$$

$$\Theta_{i,j} := \left(0.35 + \frac{j}{300}\right) \cdot \sin\left(\frac{i}{100} \cdot \pi\right) + 0.005 \cdot \sin\left(\frac{2 \cdot i}{5} \cdot \pi\right)$$

$$K_{i,j} := \left(0.4 + 0.3 \cdot \cos\left(\frac{i}{100} \cdot \pi\right)\right) \cdot \sin\left(\frac{j}{45} \cdot \pi\right)$$

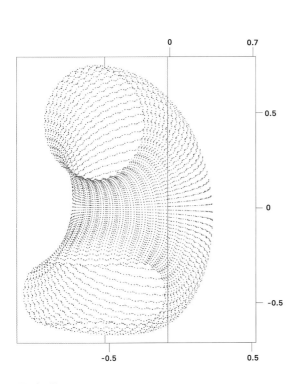

$(\Pi, \Theta, K)$

$\Theta_{i,0}$
$\Theta_{i,45}$

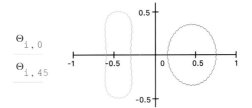

$\Pi_{i,0}, \Pi_{i,45}$

$K_{0,j}$

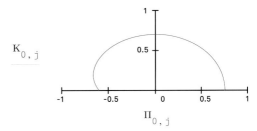

$\Pi_{0,j}$

Length: 17 mm | Width: 10 mm
Diameter: 7 mm
Cooking Time: 7 min

# COLONNE POMPEII

This ornate pasta (originally from Campania, southern Italy) is similar in shape to *fusilloni* (a large *fusilli*) but is substantially longer. *Colonne Pompeii* (columns of Pompeii) are best served with a seasoning of fresh basil, pine nuts, finely sliced garlic and olive oil, topped with a sprinkling of freshly grated Parmigiano-Reggiano.

> TWISTED LONGITUDINAL PROFILE
ⱽ SOLID CROSS-SECTION
ⱽ SMOOTH SURFACE
ⱽ SMOOTH EDGES

_ranges

$i := 0, 1 .. 10$

$j := 0, 1 .. 250$

_equations

$$\Pi_{i,j} := \mathrm{if}\left(j \le 50,\, 2 \cdot \cos\left(\frac{i}{20} \cdot \pi\right),\, 2 \cdot \cos\left(\frac{i}{20} \cdot \pi\right)\cos\left(-\frac{j}{25} \cdot \pi\right)\right) \quad \Theta_{i,j} := \mathrm{if}\left(j \le 50,\, 0,\, 2 \cdot \cos\left(\frac{i}{20} \cdot \pi\right) \cdot \sin\left(-\frac{j}{25} \cdot \pi\right) + 3 \cdot \sin\left(\frac{j-50}{200} \cdot \pi\right)\right)$$

$$K_{i,j} := \mathrm{if}\left(j \le 50,\, \sin\left(\frac{i}{20} \cdot \pi\right) + 12,\, \sin\left(\frac{i}{20} \cdot \pi\right) + \frac{6 \cdot j}{25}\right)$$

$$T_{i,j} := \mathrm{if}\left(j \le 200,\, 2 \cdot \cos\left(\frac{i}{20} \cdot \pi\right) \cdot \cos\left(-\frac{j}{25} \cdot \pi + \frac{2}{3} \cdot \pi\right),\, 2 \cdot \cos\left(\frac{i}{20} \cdot \pi\right) \cdot \sin\left(\frac{-28}{3} \cdot \pi\right)\right)$$

$$X_{i,j} := \mathrm{if}\left(j \le 200,\, 2 \cdot \cos\left(\frac{i}{20} \cdot \pi\right) \cdot \sin\left(-\frac{j}{25} \cdot \pi + \frac{2}{3} \cdot \pi\right) + 3 \cdot \sin\left(\frac{j}{200} \cdot \pi\right),\, 2 \cdot \cos\left(\frac{i}{20} \cdot \pi\right) \cdot \sin\left(\frac{-28}{3} \cdot \pi\right)\right)$$

$$\Psi_{i,j} := \mathrm{if}\left(j \le 200,\, 12 + \sin\left(\frac{i}{20} \cdot \pi\right) + \frac{6 \cdot j}{25},\, \sin\left(\frac{i}{20} \cdot \pi\right) + 60\right)$$

$$N_{i,j} := \mathrm{if}\left(j \le 200,\, 2 \cdot \cos\left(\frac{i}{20} \cdot \pi\right) \cdot \cos\left(-\frac{j}{25} \cdot \pi + \frac{4}{3} \cdot \pi\right),\, 2 \cdot \cos\left(\frac{i}{20} \cdot \pi\right) \cdot \sin\left(\frac{-28}{3} \cdot \pi\right)\right)$$

$$\Xi_{i,j} := \mathrm{if}\left(j \le 200,\, 2 \cdot \cos\left(\frac{i}{20} \cdot \pi\right) \cdot \sin\left(-\frac{j}{25} \cdot \pi + \frac{4}{3} \cdot \pi\right) + 3 \cdot \sin\left(\frac{j}{200} \cdot \pi\right),\, 2 \cdot \cos\left(\frac{i}{20} \cdot \pi\right) \cdot \sin\left(\frac{-28}{3} \cdot \pi\right)\right)$$

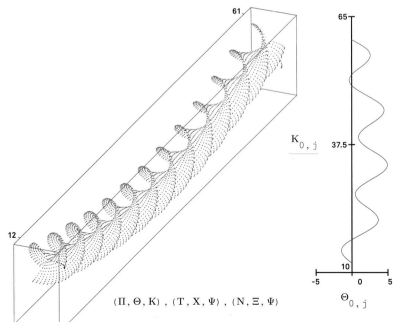

$(\Pi, \Theta, K)$ , $(T, X, \Psi)$ , $(N, \Xi, \Psi)$

$\dfrac{K_{0,j}}{\Theta_{0,j}}$

Length: 300 mm | Width: 20 mm
Cooking Time: 9 min

# CONCHIGLIE RIGATE

Shaped like their namesake, *conchiglie* (shells) exist in both *rigate* (grooved) and *lisce* (smooth) forms. Suited to light tomato sauces, ricotta cheese or *pesto genovese*, *conchiglie* hold flavourings in their grooves and cunningly designed shell. Smaller versions are used in soups, while larger shells are more commonly served with a sauce.

> PINCHED LONGITUDINAL PROFILE
⌄ SEMI-OPEN CROSS-SECTION
⌄ STRIATED SURFACE
⌄ SMOOTH EDGES

_ranges

$i := 0, 1 .. 40$

$j := 0, 1 .. 250$

_equations

$$\alpha_j := 0.25 \cdot \sin\left(\frac{j}{250} \cdot \pi\right) \cdot \cos\left(\frac{6 \cdot j + 25}{25} \cdot \pi\right) \qquad \beta_{i,j} := \frac{40 - i}{40} \cdot \left(0.3 + \sin\left(\frac{j}{250} \cdot \pi\right)\right) \cdot \pi$$

$$\gamma_{i,j} := 2.5 \cdot \cos\left(\frac{j}{125} \cdot \pi\right) + 2 \cdot \sin\left(\frac{40 - i}{80} \cdot \pi\right)^{10} \cdot \sin\left(\frac{j}{250} \cdot \pi\right)^{10} \cdot \sin\left(\frac{j}{125} \cdot \pi + 1.5 \cdot \pi\right)$$

$$\Pi_{i,j} := \alpha_j + \cos\left(\frac{j}{125} \cdot \pi\right) + \left(5 + 30 \cdot \sin\left(\frac{j}{250} \cdot \pi\right)\right) \cdot \sin(\beta_{i,j}) \cdot \sin\left[\frac{i}{40} \cdot \left[0.1 \cdot \left(1.1 + \sin\left(\frac{j}{250} \cdot \pi\right)^5\right)\right] \cdot \pi\right]$$

$$\Theta_{i,j} := \alpha_j + \left(5 + 30 \cdot \sin\left(\frac{j}{250} \cdot \pi\right)\right) \cdot \cos(\beta_{i,j}) \cdot \sin\left[\frac{i}{40} \cdot \left[0.1 \cdot \left(1.1 + \sin\left(\frac{j}{250} \cdot \pi\right)^5\right)\right] \cdot \pi\right] + \gamma_{i,j}$$

$$K_{i,j} := 25 \cdot \cos\left(\frac{j}{250} \cdot \pi\right)$$

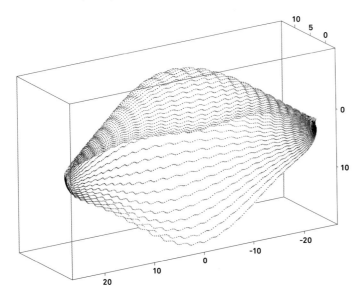

$(\Pi, \Theta, K)$

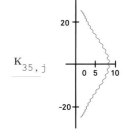

$K_{35,j}$

$\Pi_{35,j}$

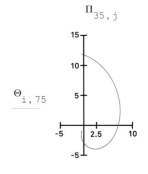

$\Theta_{i,75}$

$\Pi_{i,75}$

Length: 37 mm | Width: 23 mm
Cooking Time: 13 min

# CONCHIGLIETTE LISCE

Typically found in central and southern Italy (notably Campania), *conchigliette lisce* (small smooth shells) can be served in soups such as *minestrone*. Alternatively, these shells can accompany a meat- or vegetable-based sauce.

> <u>PI</u>NCHED LONGITUDINAL PROFILE
> ˅ <u>SE</u>MI-OPEN CROSS-SECTION
> ˅ <u>SM</u>OOTH SURFACE
> ˅ <u>SM</u>OOTH EDGES

_ranges

$i := 0, 1 .. \ 60$

$j := 0, 1 .. \ 60$

_equations

$$\alpha_{i,j} := \frac{60 - i}{60} \cdot \left(0.5 + \sin\left(\frac{j}{60} \cdot \pi\right)\right) \cdot \pi \qquad \beta_{i,j} := \frac{i}{60} \cdot \left[0.1 \cdot \left(1.1 + \sin\left(\frac{j}{60} \cdot \pi\right)^5\right)\right] \cdot \pi$$

$$\gamma_{i,j} := 2.5 \cdot \cos\left(\frac{j}{30} \cdot \pi\right) + 2 \cdot \sin\left(\frac{60 - i}{120} \cdot \pi\right)^{10} \cdot \sin\left(\frac{j}{60} \cdot \pi\right)^{10} \cdot \sin\left(\frac{j + 45}{30} \cdot \pi\right)$$

$$\Pi_{i,j} := \left(5 + 30 \cdot \sin\left(\frac{j}{60} \cdot \pi\right)\right) \cdot \sin\left(\alpha_{i,j}\right) \cdot \sin\left(\beta_{i,j}\right) + \cos\left(\frac{j}{30} \cdot \pi\right)$$

$$\Theta_{i,j} := \left(5 + 30 \cdot \sin\left(\frac{j}{60} \cdot \pi\right)\right) \cdot \cos\left(\alpha_{i,j}\right) \cdot \sin\left(\beta_{i,j}\right) + \gamma_{i,j}$$

$$K_{i,j} := 25 \cdot \cos\left(\frac{j}{60} \cdot \pi\right)$$

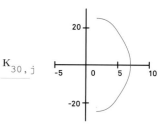

$K_{30,j}$

$\Pi_{30,j}$

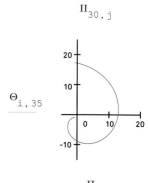

$\Theta_{i,35}$

$\Pi_{i,35}$

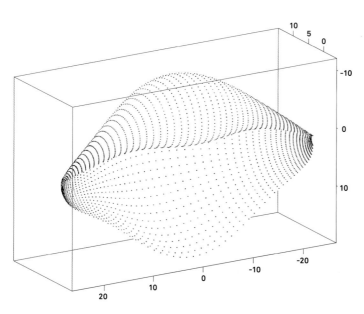

$(\Pi, \Theta, K)$

Length: 12 mm | Width: 7 mm
Cooking Time: 8 min

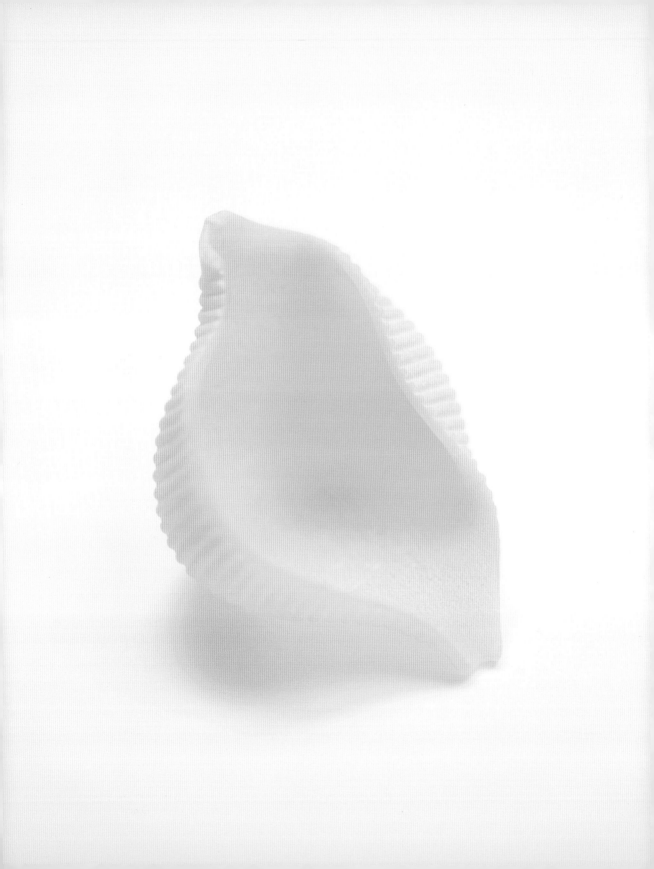

# CONCHIGLIONI RIGATI

The shape of *conchiglioni rigati* (large ribbed shells) is ideal for holding sauces and fillings (either fish or meat based) and the pasta can be baked in the oven, or placed under a grill and cooked as a gratin. *Conchiglioni rigati* are often served in the Italian-American dish *pasta primavera* (pasta in spring sauce) alongside crisp spring vegetables.

> PINCHED LONGITUDINAL PROFILE
> ⌄ SEMI-OPEN CROSS-SECTION
> ⌄ STRIATED SURFACE
> ⌄ SMOOTH EDGES

_ranges

$i := 0, 1 .. 40$

$j := 0, 1 .. 200$

_equations

$$\alpha_j := 0.25 \cdot \sin\left(\frac{j}{200} \cdot \pi\right) \cdot \cos\left(\frac{j+4}{4} \cdot \pi\right) \qquad \beta_{i,j} := \frac{i}{40} \cdot \left(0.1 + 0.1 \cdot \sin\left(\frac{j}{200} \cdot \pi\right)^6\right) \cdot \pi$$

$$\gamma_{i,j} := 2.5 \cdot \cos\left(\frac{j}{100} \cdot \pi\right) + 3 \cdot \sin\left(\frac{40-i}{80} \cdot \pi\right)^{10} \cdot \sin\left(\frac{j}{200} \cdot \pi\right)^{10} \cdot \sin\left(\frac{j+150}{100} \cdot \pi\right)$$

$$\Pi_{i,j} := \alpha_j + \left(10 + 30 \cdot \sin\left(\frac{j}{200} \cdot \pi\right)\right) \cdot \sin\left[\frac{40-i}{40} \cdot \left(0.3 + \sin\left(\frac{j}{200} \cdot \pi\right)^3\right) \cdot \pi\right] \cdot \sin(\beta_{i,j}) + \cos\left(\frac{j}{100} \cdot \pi\right)$$

$$\Theta_{i,j} := \alpha_j + \left(10 + 30 \cdot \sin\left(\frac{j}{200} \cdot \pi\right)\right) \cdot \cos\left[\frac{40-i}{40} \cdot \left(0.3 + \sin\left(\frac{j}{200} \cdot \pi\right)^3\right) \cdot \pi\right] \cdot \sin(\beta_{i,j}) + \gamma_{i,j}$$

$$K_{i,j} := 30 \cdot \cos\left(\frac{j}{200} \cdot \pi\right)$$

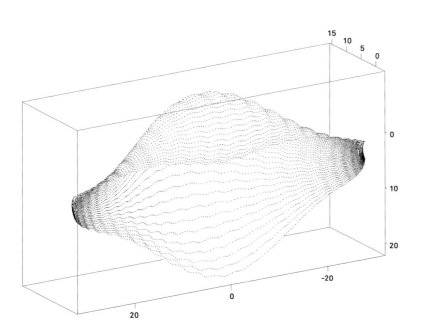

$(\Pi, \Theta, K)$

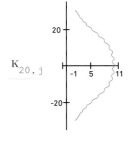

$K_{20,j}$

$\Pi_{20,j}$

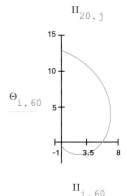

$\Theta_{i,60}$

$\Pi_{i,60}$

Length: 65 mm | Width: 36 mm
Cooking Time: 13 min

# CORALLINI LISCI

Members of the *pastine minute* (tiny pasta) group, *corallini lisci* (small smooth coral) are so called because their pierced appearance resembles the coral beads worn as jewelry in Italy. Their small size (no larger than 3.5 mm in diameter) means that *corallini* are best cooked in broths, such as Tuscan white bean soup.

› STRAIGHT LONGITUDINAL PROFILE

⌄ HOLLOW CROSS-SECTION

⌄ SMOOTH SURFACE

⌄ SMOOTH EDGES

_ranges

$i := 0, 1 .. \ 100$

$j := 0, 1 .. \ 25$

_equations

$$\Pi_{i,j} := 0.8 \cdot \cos\left(\frac{i}{50} \cdot \pi\right)$$

$$\Theta_{i,j} := 0.8 \cdot \sin\left(\frac{i}{50} \cdot \pi\right)$$

$$K_{i,j} := \frac{3 \cdot j}{50}$$

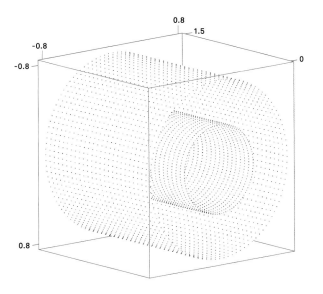

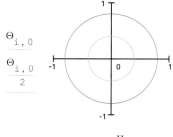

$$\left(\Pi, \Theta, K\right), \left(\frac{\Pi}{2}, \frac{\Theta}{2}, K\right)$$

Length: 4 mm | Diameter: 3 mm
Cooking Time: 11 min

# CRESTE DI GALLI

Part of the *pasta ripiena* (filled pasta) family, *creste di galli* (coxcombs) are identical to *galletti* (see page 086) except for the crest, which is smooth rather than crimped. They may be stuffed, cooked and served in a simple *marinara* (mariner's) sauce, which contains tomato, garlic and basil.

> BENT LONGITUDINAL PROFILE

ᵛ HOLLOW CROSS-SECTION

ᵛ SMOOTH SURFACE

ᵛ SMOOTH EDGES

_ranges

$i := 0, 1 .. 140$

$j := 0, 1 .. 70$

_equations

$$f(x) := \left[ \frac{1 + \sin[(1.5 + x) \cdot \pi]}{2} \right]^5$$

$$\alpha_{i,j} := 0.3 \cdot \sin\left( f\left(\frac{i}{140}\right) \cdot \pi + 0.5 \cdot \pi \right)^{1000} \cdot \cos\left(\frac{j}{70} \cdot \pi\right) \qquad \beta_{i,j} := 0.3 \cdot \cos\left( f\left(\frac{i}{140}\right) \cdot \pi \right)^{1000} \cdot \sin\left(\frac{j}{70} \cdot \pi\right)$$

$$\Pi_{i,j} := \left( 0.5 + 0.3 \cdot \cos\left( f\left(\frac{i}{140}\right) \cdot 2 \cdot \pi \right) \right) \cdot \cos\left(\frac{j}{70} \cdot \pi\right) + 0.15 \cdot \left(\frac{j}{70}\right)^{10} \cdot \cos\left( f\left(\frac{i}{140}\right) \cdot 2 \cdot \pi \right)^3 + \alpha_{i,j}$$

$$\Theta_{i,j} := 0.35 \cdot \sin\left( f\left(\frac{i}{140}\right) \cdot 2 \cdot \pi \right) + 0.15 \cdot \frac{j}{70} \cdot \sin\left( f\left(\frac{i}{140}\right) \cdot 2 \cdot \pi \right)$$

$$K_{i,j} := \left( 0.4 + 0.3 \cdot \cos\left( f\left(\frac{i}{140}\right) \cdot 2 \cdot \pi \right) \right) \cdot \sin\left(\frac{j}{70} \cdot \pi\right) + \beta_{i,j}$$

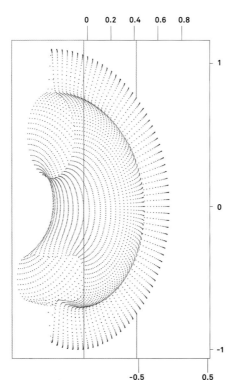

$(\Pi, \Theta, K)$

$\dfrac{\Theta_{i,0}}{\Theta_{i,50}}$

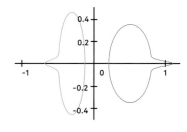

$\Pi_{i,0}, \Pi_{i,50}$

$\dfrac{K_{0,j}}{}$

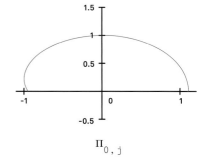

$\Pi_{0,j}$

Length: 36 mm | Width: 20 mm
Diameter: 8 mm
Cooking Time: 14 min

# CUORETTI

A romantically shaped scion of the *pastine minute* (tiny pasta) clan, *cuoretti* (tiny hearts) are minuscule. In fact, along with *acini di pepe* (page 015), they are one of the smallest forms of pasta. Like all *pastine* they may be served in soup, such as cream of chicken.

> STRAIGHT LONGITUDINAL PROFILE
ˇ SOLID CROSS-SECTION
ˇ SMOOTH SURFACE
ˇ SMOOTH EDGES

_ranges

$i := 0, 1 .. \ 300$

$j := 0, 1 .. \ 10$

_equations

$$\Pi_{i,j} := 2\cos\left(\frac{i}{150}\cdot\pi\right) - \cos\left(\frac{i}{75}\cdot\pi\right) - \sin\left(\frac{i}{300}\cdot\pi\right)^{150} - \left(\left|\cos\left(\frac{i}{300}\cdot\pi\right)\right|\right)^{5}$$

$$\Theta_{i,j} := 2\cdot\sin\left(\frac{i}{150}\cdot\pi\right) - \sin\left(\frac{i}{75}\cdot\pi\right)$$

$$K_{i,j} := \frac{j}{10}$$

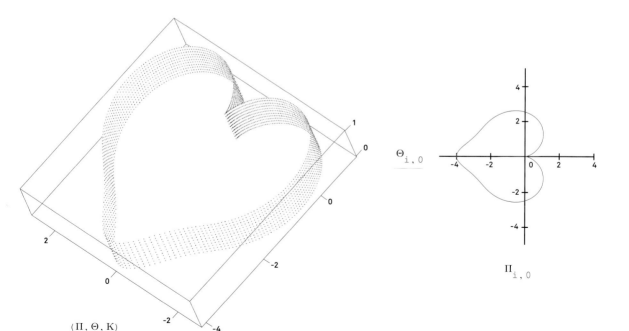

$(\Pi, \Theta, K)$

$\Theta_{i,0}$

$\Pi_{i,0}$

Length: 4 mm | Width: 3 mm
Cooking Time: 5 min

# DITALI RIGATI

Another speciality of the Campania region of southern Italy, *ditali rigati* (grooved thimbles) are compact and typically less than 10 mm long. Like other *pastine*, they are usually found in soups such as *pasta e patate*. Their stocky shape makes them a sustaining winter snack, as well as an excellent addition to salads.

> STRAIGHT LONGITUDINAL PROFILE
> ⌄ HOLLOW CROSS-SECTION
> ⌄ STRIATED SURFACE
> ⌄ SMOOTH EDGES

_ranges

$i := 0, 1 .. 200$

$j := 0, 1 .. 25$

_equations

$$\Pi_{i,j} := \cos\left(\frac{i}{100} \cdot \pi\right) + 0.03 \cdot \cos\left(\frac{7 \cdot i}{40} \cdot \pi\right) + 0.25 \cdot \cos\left(\frac{j}{50} \cdot \pi\right)$$

$$\Theta_{i,j} := 1.1 \cdot \sin\left(\frac{i}{100} \cdot \pi\right) + 0.03 \cdot \sin\left(\frac{7 \cdot i}{40} \cdot \pi\right) + 0.25 \cdot \sin\left(\frac{j}{50} \cdot \pi\right)$$

$$\mathrm{K}_{i,j} := \frac{j}{10}$$

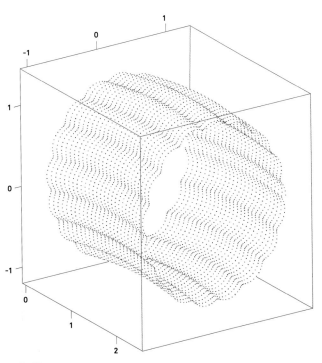

$(\Pi, \Theta, \mathrm{K})$

$\underline{\Theta_{i,0}}$

$\Pi_{i,0}$

Length: 9 mm | Diameter: 8 mm
Cooking Time: 12 min

# FAGOTTINI

A notable member of the *pasta ripiena* (filled pasta) family, *fagottini* (little purses) are made from circles of durum-wheat dough. A spoonful of ricotta, steamed vegetables or even stewed fruit is placed on the dough, and the corners are then pinched together to form a bundle. These packed dumplings are similar to *ravioli*, only larger.

> PINCHED LONGITUDINAL PROFILE
⌄ HOLLOW CROSS-SECTION
⌄ SMOOTH SURFACE
⌄ SMOOTH EDGES

_ranges

$i := 0, 1 .. \ 200$

$j := 0, 1 .. \ 50$

_equations

$$\alpha_{i,j} := \left[ \left( 0.8 + \sin\left(\frac{i}{100} \cdot \pi\right)^8 - 0.8 \cdot \cos\left(\frac{i}{25} \cdot \pi\right) \right)^{1.5} + 0.2 + 0.2 \cdot \sin\left(\frac{i}{100} \cdot \pi\right) \right]$$

$$\beta_{i,j} := \left[ \left( 0.9 + \cos\left(\frac{i}{100} \cdot \pi\right)^8 - 0.9 \cdot \cos\left(\frac{i}{25} \cdot \pi + 0.03 \cdot \pi\right) \right)^{1.5} + 0.3 \cdot \left(\cos\left(\frac{i}{100} \cdot \pi\right)\right) \right]$$

$$\gamma_{i,j} := 4 - \frac{4 \cdot j}{500} \cdot \left( 1 + \cos\left(\frac{i}{100} \cdot \pi\right)^8 - 0.8 \cos\left(\frac{i}{25} \cdot \pi\right) \right)^{1.5}$$

$$\Pi_{i,j} := \cos\left(\frac{i}{100} \cdot \pi\right) \cdot \left[ \alpha_{i,j} \cdot \sin\left(\frac{j}{100} \cdot \pi\right)^8 + 0.6 \left( 2 + \sin\left(\frac{i}{100} \cdot \pi\right)^2 \right) \cdot \sin\left(\frac{j}{50} \cdot \pi\right)^2 \right]$$

$$\Theta_{i,j} := \sin\left(\frac{i}{100} \cdot \pi\right) \cdot \left[ \beta_{i,j} \cdot \sin\left(\frac{j}{100} \cdot \pi\right)^8 + 0.6 \left( 2 + \cos\left(\frac{i}{100} \cdot \pi\right)^2 \right) \cdot \sin\left(\frac{j}{50} \cdot \pi\right)^2 \right]$$

$$K_{i,j} := \left( 1 + \sin\left(\frac{j}{100} \cdot \pi - 0.5 \cdot \pi\right) \right) \cdot \left[ \gamma_{i,j} - \frac{4 \cdot j}{500} \left( 1 + \sin\left(\frac{i}{100} \cdot \pi\right)^8 - 0.8 \cos\left(\frac{i}{25} \cdot \pi\right) \right)^{1.5} \right]$$

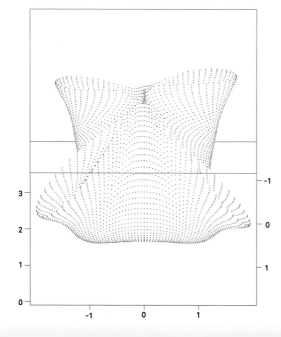

$(\Pi, \Theta, K)$

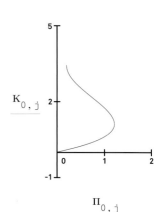

$\underline{K_{0,j}}$

$\Pi_{0,j}$

Length: 30 mm | Width: 30 mm
Cooking Time: 4 min

# FARFALLE

A mixture of durum-wheat flour, eggs and water, *farfalle* (butterflies) come from the Emilia-Romagna and Lombardy regions of northern Italy. They are best served in a rich *carbonara* sauce (made with cream, eggs and bacon). Depending on size, *farfalle* might be accompanied by green peas and chicken or ham.

> PINCHED LONGITUDINAL PROFILE
∨ SOLID CROSS-SECTION
∨ SMOOTH SURFACE
∨ CRENELLATED EDGES

_ranges

$i := 0, 1 .. 80$

$j := 0, 1 .. 80$

_equations

$$\alpha_i := \sin\left(\frac{7 \cdot i + 16}{40} \cdot \pi\right) \qquad \beta_{i,j} := \frac{7 \cdot j}{16} + 4 \cdot \sin\left(\frac{i}{80} \cdot \pi\right) \cdot \sin\left(\frac{j - 10}{120} \cdot \pi\right)$$

$$\gamma_{i,j} := 10 \cdot \cos\left(\frac{i + 80}{80} \cdot \pi\right) \cdot \sin\left(\frac{j + 110}{100} \cdot \pi\right)^9 \qquad \eta_{i,j} := \frac{7 \cdot j}{16} - 4 \cdot \sin\left(\frac{i}{80} \cdot \pi\right) - \alpha_i \cdot \sin\left(\frac{10 - j}{20} \cdot \pi\right)$$

$$\Pi_{i,j} := \frac{3 \cdot i}{8} + \text{if}\left(20 \le i \le 60, 7 \cdot \sin\left(\frac{i + 40}{40} \cdot \pi\right)^3 \cdot \sin\left(\frac{j + 110}{100} \cdot \pi\right)^9, \gamma_{i,j}\right)$$

$$\Theta_{i,j} := \text{if}\left(10 \le j \le 70, \beta_{i,j} - 4 \cdot \sin\left(\frac{i}{80} \cdot \pi\right) \cdot \sin\left(\frac{70 - j}{120} \cdot \pi\right), \text{if}\left(j \le 10, \eta_{i,j}, \iota_{i,j}\right)\right)$$

$$K_{i,j} := 3 \cdot \sin\left(\frac{i + 10}{20} \cdot \pi\right) \cdot \sin\left(\frac{j}{80} \cdot \pi\right)^{1.5}$$

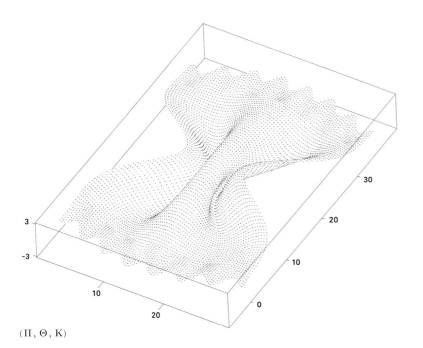

$(\Pi, \Theta, K)$

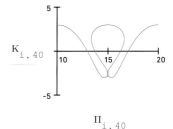

$\dfrac{K_{i,40}}{\Pi_{i,40}}$

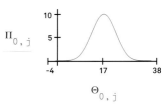

$\dfrac{\Pi_{0,j}}{\Theta_{0,j}}$

Length: 41 mm | Width: 30 mm
Cooking Time: 12 min

# FARFALLINE

The small size of this well-known member of the *pastine minute* (tiny pasta) lineage means that *farfalline* (tiny butterflies), are suitable for light soups, such as *pomodori e robiola* (a mixture of tomato and soft cheese). A crimped pasta cutter and a central pinch create the iconic shape.

› PINCHED LONGITUDINAL PROFILE

ᵛ SOLID CROSS-SECTION

ᵛ SMOOTH SURFACE

ᵛ CRENELLATED EDGES

_ranges

$i := 0, 1 .. 250$

$j := 0, 1 .. 50$

_equations

$$\alpha_i := 30\cos\left(\frac{i}{125}\cdot\pi\right) + 0.5\cdot\cos\left(\frac{6\cdot i}{25}\cdot\pi\right) \qquad \beta_i := 30\cdot\sin\left(\frac{i}{125}\cdot\pi\right) + 0.5\cdot\sin\left(\frac{6\cdot i}{25}\cdot\pi\right)$$

$$\Pi_{i,j} := \cos\left(\frac{3\cdot\alpha_i}{100}\cdot\pi\right)$$

$$\Theta_{i,j} := 0.5\cdot\sin\left(\frac{3\cdot\alpha_i}{100}\cdot\pi\right)\cdot\left(1 + \sin\left(\frac{j}{100}\cdot\pi\right)\right)^{10}$$

$$K_{i,j} := \frac{\beta_i\cdot j}{500}$$

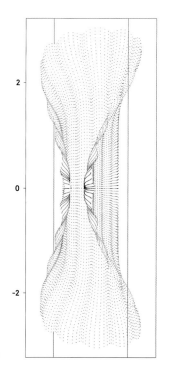

$(\Pi, \Theta, K)$

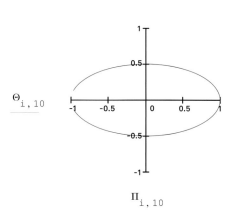

$\Theta_{i,10}$

$\Pi_{i,10}$

Length: 14 mm | Width: 7 mm
Cooking Time: 6 min

# FARFALLONI

Like *farfalle*, *farfalloni* (large butterflies) are well matched by a tomato- or butter-based sauce with peas and ham. They are also perfect with marrow vegetables such as roast courgette or puréed pumpkin, topped with Parmigiano-Reggiano and a sprinkling of *noce moscata* (nutmeg).

> PINCHED LONGITUDINAL PROFILE
>> SOLID CROSS-SECTION
>>> SMOOTH SURFACE
>>>> CRENELLATED EDGES

_ranges

$i := 0, 1 .. 70$

$j := 0, 1 .. 70$

_equations

$$\alpha_{i,j} := 10 \cdot \cos\left(\frac{i+70}{70} \cdot \pi\right) \cdot \sin\left(\frac{2 \cdot j}{175} \cdot \pi + 1.1 \cdot \pi\right)^9 \qquad \beta_j := 0.3 \cdot \sin\left(\frac{6 \cdot j}{7} \cdot \pi + 0.4 \cdot \pi\right)$$

$$\gamma_{i,j} := \mathrm{if}\left(17 \le i \le 52, \, 7 \cdot \sin\left(\frac{i+35}{35} \cdot \pi\right)^3 \cdot \sin\left(\frac{2 \cdot j}{175} \cdot \pi + 1.1 \cdot \pi\right)^9, \, \alpha_{i,j}\right)$$

$$\iota_{i,j} := \frac{j}{2} + 4 \cdot \sin\left(\frac{i}{70} \cdot \pi\right) \cdot \sin\left(\frac{j-10}{100} \cdot \pi\right) - 4 \cdot \sin\left(\frac{i}{70} \cdot \pi\right) \cdot \sin\left(\frac{60-j}{100} \cdot \pi\right)$$

$$\lambda_{i,j} := \frac{j}{2} + 4 \cdot \sin\left(\frac{i}{70} \cdot \pi\right) + 0.3 \cdot \sin\left(\frac{2 \cdot i + 2.8}{7} \cdot \pi\right) \cdot \sin\left(\frac{j-60}{20} \cdot \pi\right)$$

$$\mu_{i,j} := \frac{j}{2} - 4 \cdot \sin\left(\frac{i}{70} \cdot \pi\right) - 0.3 \cdot \sin\left(\frac{2 \cdot i + 2.8}{7} \cdot \pi\right) \cdot \sin\left(\frac{10-j}{20} \cdot \pi\right)$$

$$\Pi_{i,j} := \frac{3 \cdot i}{7} + \gamma_{i,j} \qquad \Theta_{i,j} := \mathrm{if}\left(10 \le j \le 60, \, \iota_{i,j}, \, \mathrm{if}\left(j \le 10, \, \mu_{i,j}, \, \lambda_{i,j}\right)\right)$$

$$K_{i,j} := 3 \cdot \sin\left(\frac{2 \cdot i + 17.5}{35} \cdot \pi\right) \cdot \sin\left(\frac{j}{70} \cdot \pi\right)^{1.5}$$

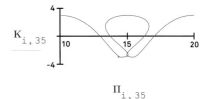

$K_{i,35}$

$\Pi_{i,35}$

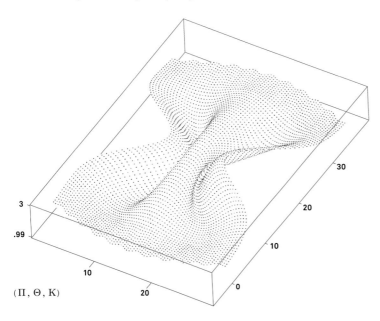

$(\Pi, \Theta, K)$

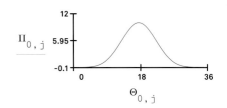

$\Pi_{0,j}$

$\Theta_{0,j}$

Length: 50 mm | Width: 34 mm
Cooking Time: 11 min

# FESTONATI

This smooth member of the *pasta corta* (short pasta) family is named after 'festoons' (decorative lengths of fabric with the rippled profile of a garland). *Festonati* can be served with grilled aubergine or home-grown tomatoes, topped with grated scamorza, fresh basil, olive oil, garlic and red chilli flakes.

> STRAIGHT LONGITUDINAL PROFILE
> ⌄ HOLLOW CROSS-SECTION
> ⌄ STRIATED SURFACE
> ⌄ SMOOTH EDGES

_ranges

$i := 0, 1 .. 100$

$j := 0, 1 .. 100$

_equations

$$\Pi_{i,j} := 5 \cdot \cos\left(\frac{i}{50} \cdot \pi\right) + 0.5 \cdot \cos\left(\frac{i}{50} \cdot \pi\right) \cdot \left(1 + \sin\left(\frac{j}{100} \cdot \pi\right)\right) + 0.5 \cdot \cos\left(\frac{i+25}{25} \cdot \pi\right) \cdot \left(1 + \sin\left(\frac{j}{5} \cdot \pi\right)\right)$$

$$\Theta_{i,j} := 5 \cdot \sin\left(\frac{i}{50} \cdot \pi\right) + 0.5 \cdot \sin\left(\frac{i}{50} \cdot \pi\right) \cdot \left(1 + \sin\left(\frac{j}{100} \cdot \pi\right)\right) + 0.5 \cdot \sin\left(\frac{i}{25} \cdot \pi\right) \cdot \left(1 + \sin\left(\frac{j}{5} \cdot \pi\right)\right)$$

$$K_{i,j} := \frac{j}{2} + 2 \cdot \sin\left(\frac{3 \cdot i + 25}{50} \cdot \pi\right)$$

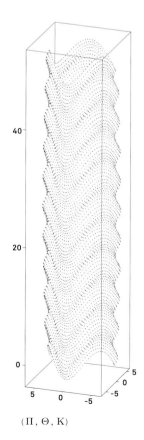

$(\Pi, \Theta, K)$

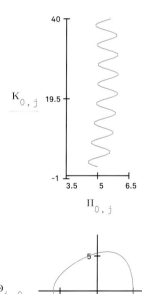

$K_{0,j}$

$\Pi_{0,j}$

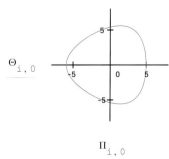

$\Theta_{i,0}$

$\Pi_{i,0}$

Length: 46 mm | Width: 15 mm
Cooking Time: 10 min

# FETTUCCINE

This famous *pasta lunga* (long pasta) is made with durum-wheat flour, water and, in the case of *fettuccine all'uovo*, eggs ideally within days of laying. *Fettuccine* (little ribbons) hail from the Lazio region. Popular in many dishes, they are an ideal accompaniment to *Alfredo* sauce: a rich mix of cream, parmesan, garlic and parsley.

› BENT LONGITUDINAL PROFILE
⌄ SOLID CROSS-SECTION
⌄ SMOOTH SURFACE
⌄ SMOOTH EDGES

_ranges

$i := 0, 1 .. 150$

$j := 0, 1 .. 10$

_equations

$$\Pi_{i,j} := 1.8 \cdot \sin\left(\frac{4 \cdot i}{375} \cdot \pi\right)$$

$$\Theta_{i,j} := 1.6 \cdot \cos\left(\frac{6 \cdot i}{375} \cdot \pi\right) \cdot \sin\left(\frac{3 \cdot i}{750} \cdot \pi\right)$$

$$K_{i,j} := \frac{i}{75} + \frac{j}{20}$$

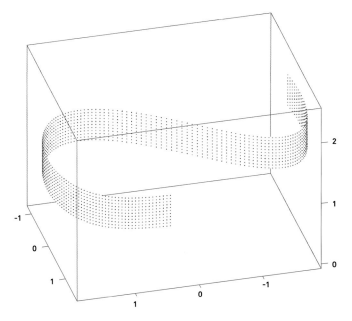

$(\Pi, \Theta, K)$

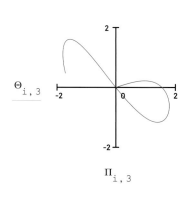

$\Theta_{i,3}$

$\Pi_{i,3}$

Length: **150 mm** | Width: **7 mm**
Cooking Time: **3 min**

# FIOCCHI RIGATI

A distant relative of the *farfalle* family, *fiocchi rigati* (grooved flakes) are smaller than either *farfalloni* or *farfalle*, but larger than *farfalline*. Their corrugated surface collects more sauce than a typical *farfalle*. For a more unusual dish, *fiocchi rigati* can be served in a tomato and vodka sauce.

> PINCHED LONGITUDINAL PROFILE
⌄ SOLID CROSS-SECTION
⌄ STRIATED SURFACE
⌄ SMOOTH EDGES

_ranges

$i := 0, 1 .. 80$

$j := 0, 1 .. 80$

_equations

$$\alpha_{i,j} := 10 \cdot \cos\left(\frac{i+80}{80} \cdot \pi\right) \cdot \sin\left(\frac{j+110}{100} \cdot \pi\right)^9$$

$$\beta_{i,j} := \frac{35 \cdot j}{80} + 4 \cdot \sin\left(\frac{i}{80} \cdot \pi\right) \cdot \sin\left(\frac{j-10}{120} \cdot \pi\right)$$

$$\Pi_{i,j} := \frac{30 \cdot i}{80} + \text{if}\left(20 \le i \le 60, 7 \cdot \sin\left(\frac{i+40}{40} \cdot \pi\right)^3 \cdot \sin\left(\frac{j+110}{100} \cdot \pi\right)^9, \alpha_{i,j}\right)$$

$$\Theta_{i,j} := \beta_{i,j} - 4 \cdot \sin\left(\frac{i}{80} \cdot \pi\right) \cdot \sin\left(\frac{70-j}{120} \cdot \pi\right)$$

$$K_{i,j} := 3 \cdot \sin\left(\frac{i+10}{20} \pi\right) \cdot \sin\left(\frac{j}{80} \cdot \pi\right)^{1.5} - 0.7 \cdot \left[\frac{\left(\sin\left(\frac{3 \cdot j}{8} \cdot \pi\right) + 1\right)}{2}\right]^4$$

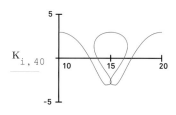

$\frac{K_{i,40}}{\Pi_{i,40}}$

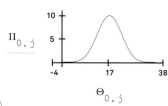

$\frac{\Pi_{0,j}}{\Theta_{0,j}}$

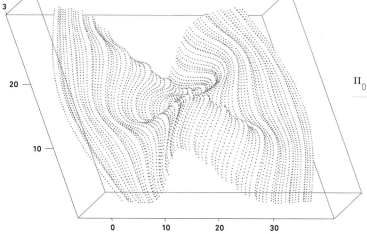

$(\Pi, \Theta, K)$

Length: 33 mm | Width: 23 mm
Cooking Time: 12 min

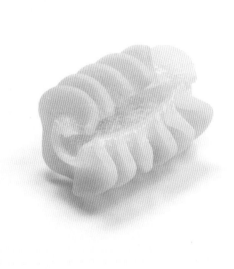

# FISARMONICHE

Named after the accordion – whose bellows their bunched profiles recall – *fisarmoniche* are perfect for capturing thick sauces, which cling to their folds. This sturdy pasta is said to have been invented in the fifteenth century, in the Italian town of Loreto in the Marche, east central Italy.

› BUNCHED LONGITUDINAL PROFILE
  ˅ SEMI-OPEN CROSS-SECTION
    ˅ SMOOTH SURFACE
      ˅ CRENELLATED EDGES

_ranges

$i := 0, 1 .. \ 70$

$j := 0, 1 .. \ 1000$

_equations

$$\Pi_{i,j} := \left[ 1.5 + 3 \cdot \left( \frac{i}{70} \right)^5 + 4 \cdot \sin\left( \frac{j}{200} \cdot \pi \right)^{50} \right] \cdot \cos\left( \frac{4 \cdot i}{175} \cdot \pi \right)$$

$$\Theta_{i,j} := \left[ 1.5 + 3 \cdot \left( \frac{i}{70} \right)^5 + 4 \cdot \sin\left( \frac{j}{200} \cdot \pi \right)^{50} \right] \cdot \sin\left( \frac{4 \cdot i}{175} \cdot \pi \right)$$

$$K_{i,j} := \frac{j}{50} + \cos\left( \frac{3 \cdot i}{14} \cdot \pi \right) \cdot \sin\left( \frac{j}{1000} \cdot \pi \right)$$

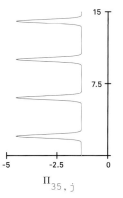

$K_{35,j}$

$\Pi_{35,j}$

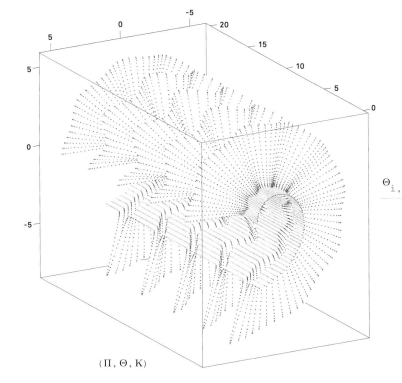

$(\Pi, \Theta, K)$

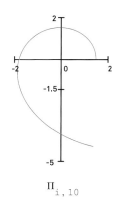

$\Theta_{i,10}$

$\Pi_{i,10}$

Length: 23 mm | Width: 16 mm
Cooking Time: 10 min

# FUNGHINI

The modest dimensions of this *pastine minute* (tiny pasta) make *funghini* (little mushrooms) especially suitable for soups, such as a *minestrone* made from chopped and sautéed celeriac.

> PINCHED LONGITUDINAL PROFILE
> ⌄ SOLID CROSS-SECTION
> ⌄ SMOOTH SURFACE
> ⌄ CRENELLATED EDGES

_ranges

$i := 0, 1 .. 300$

$j := 0, 1 .. 30$

_equations

$$\alpha_{i,j} := 5\cdot\cos\left(\frac{i}{150}\cdot\pi\right) + 0.05\cdot\cos\left(\frac{i}{3}\cdot\pi\right)\cdot\sin\left(\frac{j}{60}\cdot\pi\right)^{2000} \qquad \beta_{i,j} := \frac{j}{30}\cdot\left(5\cdot\sin\left(\frac{i}{150}\cdot\pi\right) + 0.05\cdot\sin\left(\frac{i}{3}\cdot\pi\right)\right)$$

$$\gamma_{i,j} := \frac{j}{10}\left(2\cdot\sin\left(\frac{i}{150}\cdot\pi\right) + 0.05\cdot\sin\left(\frac{i}{3}\cdot\pi\right)\right) \qquad \zeta_{i,j} := \mathrm{if}\left(i \le 150, \beta_{i,j}, \mathrm{if}\left(j \le 10, \gamma_{i,j}, 2\cdot\sin\left(\frac{i}{150}\cdot\pi\right) + 0.05\cdot\sin\left(\frac{i}{6}\cdot\pi\right)\right)\right)$$

$$\Pi_{i,j} := 0.05\cdot\cos\left(\frac{\alpha_{i,j}}{5}\cdot\pi\right) + 0.3\cdot\cos\left(\frac{\alpha_{i,j}}{5}\cdot\pi\right)\cdot\sin\left(\frac{3\cdot\zeta_{i,j}}{50}\cdot\pi\right)^2$$

$$\Theta_{i,j} := 0.01\cdot\sin\left(\frac{\alpha_{i,j}}{5}\cdot\pi\right) + 0.3\cdot\sin\left(\frac{\alpha_{i,j}}{5}\cdot\pi\right)\cdot\sin\left(\frac{3\cdot\zeta_{i,j}}{50}\cdot\pi\right)^2$$

$$K_{i,j} := 0.25\cdot\sin\left(\frac{\zeta_{i,j}+3}{10}\cdot\pi\right)$$

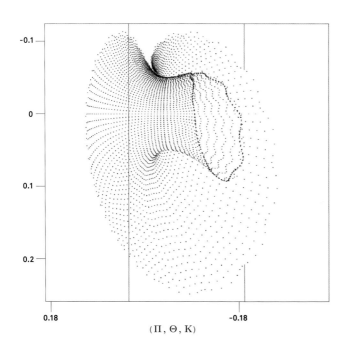

$(\Pi, \Theta, K)$

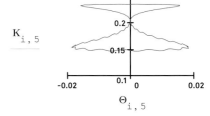

$K_{i,5}$

$\Theta_{i,5}$

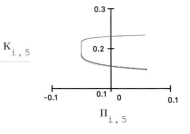

$K_{i,5}$

$\Pi_{i,5}$

Length: 8 mm | Width: 7 mm
Cooking Time: 6 min

# FUSILLI

A popular set from the *pasta corta* (short pasta) family, *fusilli* (little spindles) were originally made by quickly wrapping a *spaghetto* (see page 165) around a large needle. Best served as *pastasciutta* (pasta boiled and drained) with a creamy sauce containing slices of spicy sausage.

> TWISTED LONGITUDINAL PROFILE
>  ⌄ SOLID CROSS-SECTION
>   ⌄ SMOOTH SURFACE
>    ⌄ SMOOTH EDGES

_ranges

$i := 0, 1 .. \ 200$

$j := 0, 1 .. \ 25$

_equations

$$\Pi_{i,j} := 6 \cdot \cos\left(\frac{3 \cdot i + 10}{100} \cdot \pi\right) \cdot \cos\left(\frac{j}{25} \cdot \pi\right)$$

$$\Theta_{i,j} := 6 \cdot \sin\left(\frac{3 \cdot i + 10}{100} \cdot \pi\right) \cdot \cos\left(\frac{j}{25} \cdot \pi\right)$$

$$K_{i,j} := \frac{3 \cdot i}{20} + 2.5 \cdot \cos\left(\frac{j + 12.5}{25} \cdot \pi\right)$$

$\dfrac{K_{20,j}}{\Pi_{20,j}}$

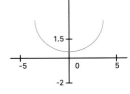

$\dfrac{K_{i,0}}{\Theta_{i,0}}$

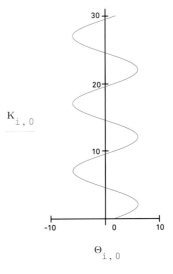

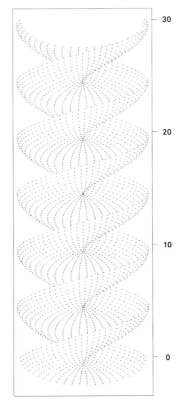

$(\Pi, \Theta, K)$

Length: 33 mm | Width: 10 mm
Cooking Time: 12 min

# FUSILLI AL FERRETTO

To create this Neapolitan variety of *fusilli*, a small amount of durum-wheat flour is kneaded and placed along a *ferretto* (small iron stick) that is then rolled between the hands to create a thick irregular twist of dough. The shape is removed and left to dry on a wicker tray known as a *spasa*. *Fusilli al ferretto* are best dished up with lamb *ragù*.

> TWISTED LONGITUDINAL PROFILE

⌄ SOLID CROSS-SECTION

⌄ SMOOTH SURFACE

⌄ SMOOTH EDGES

_ranges

$i := 0, 1 .. 140$

$j := 0, 1 .. 40$

_equations

$$\alpha_{i,j} := \frac{6 \cdot i}{7} + 15 \cdot \cos\left(\frac{j}{20} \cdot \pi\right)$$

$$\Pi_{i,j} := \left(3 + 1.5 \cdot \sin\left(\frac{i}{140} \cdot \pi\right)^{0.5} \cdot \sin\left(\frac{j}{20} \cdot \pi\right)\right) \cdot \sin\left(\frac{13 \cdot i}{280} \cdot \pi\right) + 5 \cdot \sin\left(\frac{2 \cdot \alpha_{i,j}}{135} \cdot \pi\right)$$

$$\Theta_{i,j} := \left(3 + 1.5 \cdot \sin\left(\frac{i}{140} \cdot \pi\right)^{0.5} \cdot \sin\left(\frac{j}{20} \cdot \pi\right)\right) \cdot \cos\left(\frac{13 \cdot i}{280} \cdot \pi\right)$$

$$K_{i,j} := \alpha_{i,j}$$

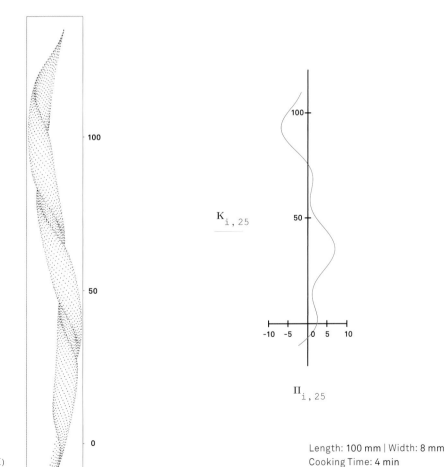

$(\Pi, \Theta, K)$

$K_{i,25}$

$\Pi_{i,25}$

Length: 100 mm | Width: 8 mm
Cooking Time: 4 min

# FUSILLI CAPRI

A longer and more compact regional adaptation of *fusilli*, *fusilli Capri* are suited to a hearty *ragù* of lamb or pork sausages, or may also be combined with rocket and lemon to form a lighter dish.

> TWISTED LONGITUDINAL PROFILE
> ⌄ SOLID CROSS-SECTION
> ⌄ SMOOTH SURFACE
> ⌄ SMOOTH EDGES

_ranges

$i := 0, 1 .. 150$

$j := 0, 1 .. 50$

_equations

$$\Pi_{i,j} := 6 \cdot \cos\left(\frac{j}{50} \cdot \pi\right) \cos\left(\frac{i + 2.5}{25} \cdot \pi\right)$$

$$\Theta_{i,j} := 6 \cdot \cos\left(\frac{j}{50} \cdot \pi\right) \cdot \sin\left(\frac{i + 2.5}{25} \cdot \pi\right)$$

$$K_{i,j} := \frac{2 \cdot i}{3} + 14 \cdot \cos\left(\frac{j + 25}{50} \cdot \pi\right)$$

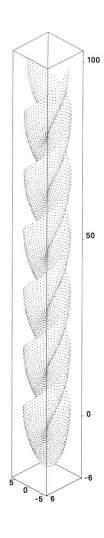

$(\Pi, \Theta, K)$

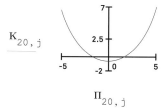

$K_{20,j}$

$\Pi_{20,j}$

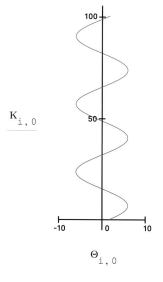

$K_{i,0}$

$\Theta_{i,0}$

Length: 170 mm | Width: 16 mm
Cooking Time: 9 min

# FUSILLI LUNGHI BUCATI

A distinctive member of the extended *fusilli* clan, *fusilli lunghi bucati* (long pierced *fusilli*) originated in Campania, southern Italy, and have a spring-like profile. Like all *fusilli* they are traditionally consumed with a meat-based *ragù*, but may also be combined with thick vegetable sauces and baked in the oven.

› TWISTED LONGITUDINAL PROFILE

˅ HOLLOW CROSS-SECTION

˅ SMOOTH SURFACE

˅ SMOOTH EDGES

_ranges

$i := 0, 1 .. \ 20$

$j := 0, 1 .. \ 200$

_equations

$$\alpha_{i,j} := 10 + \cos\left(\frac{i}{10} \cdot \pi\right) + 2\cdot\cos\left(\frac{j+10}{10} \cdot \pi\right) + 10\cdot\cos\left(\frac{j+140}{160} \cdot \pi\right)$$

$$\beta_{i,j} := 20 + \cos\left(\frac{i}{10} \cdot \pi\right) + 2\cdot\cos\left(\frac{j+10}{10} \cdot \pi\right) \qquad \gamma_{i,j} := \frac{j+10}{10}\cdot\pi \qquad \zeta_{i,j} := \frac{i}{10}\cdot\pi$$

$$\eta_{i,j} := 7 + 20\cdot\sin\left(\frac{j-20}{160} \cdot \pi\right) \qquad \iota_{i,j} := 70\cdot\left(0.1 - \frac{j-180}{200}\right)$$

$$\Pi_{i,j} := if\left(20 \leq j \leq 180, \alpha_{i,j}, if\left(j \leq 20, \cos\left(\zeta_{i,j}\right) + 2\cdot\cos\left(\gamma_{i,j}\right), \beta_{i,j}\right)\right)$$

$$\Theta_{i,j} := if\left(20 \leq j \leq 180, \sin\left(\zeta_{i,j}\right) + 2\cdot\sin\left(\gamma_{i,j}\right), \sin\left(\zeta_{i,j}\right) + 2\cdot\sin\left(\gamma_{i,j}\right)\right)$$

$$K_{i,j} := if\left(20 \leq j \leq 180, \eta_{i,j}, if\left(j \leq 20, \frac{7\cdot j}{20}, \iota_{i,j}\right)\right)$$

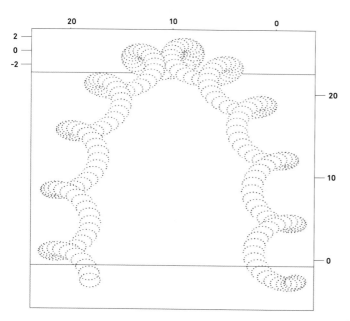

$(\Pi, \Theta, K)$

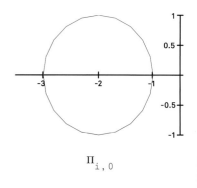

$\dfrac{\Theta_{i,0}}{\Pi_{i,0}}$

Length: 210 mm | Width: 27 mm
Diameter: 3 mm
Cooking Time: 14 min

# GALLETTI

According to their maker, Barilla, the origin of *galletti* (small cocks) is uncertain, but their shape recalls that of the *chifferi* (see page 043) with the addition of an undulating crest. *Galletti* are usually served in tomato sauces, but combine equally well with a *boscaiola* (woodsman's) sauce of mushrooms. See also *creste di galli* (page 054).

> BENT LONGITUDINAL PROFILE
∨ HOLLOW CROSS-SECTION
∨ STRIATED SURFACE
∨ SMOOTH EDGES

_ranges

$i := 0, 1 .. 140$

$j := 0, 1 .. 70$

_equations

$$f(x) := \left(\frac{1 + \sin(x \cdot \pi + 1.5 \cdot \pi)}{2}\right)^5$$

$$\alpha_{i,j} := 0.4 \cdot \sin\left(f\left(\frac{i}{140}\right) \cdot \pi + 0.5 \cdot \pi\right)^{1000} \cdot \cos\left(\frac{j}{70} \cdot \pi\right)$$

$$\beta_{i,j} := 0.15 \cdot \sin\left(f\left(\frac{i}{140}\right) \cdot \pi + 0.5 \cdot \pi\right)^{1000} \cdot \cos\left(\frac{j}{7} \cdot \pi\right)$$

$$\gamma_{i,j} := 0.4 \cdot \cos\left(f\left(\frac{i}{140}\right) \cdot \pi\right)^{1000} \cdot \sin\left(\frac{j}{70} \cdot \pi\right)$$

$$\Pi_{i,j} := \left(0.5 + 0.3 \cdot \cos\left(f\left(\frac{i}{140}\right) \cdot 2 \cdot \pi\right)\right) \cdot \cos\left(\frac{j}{70} \cdot \pi\right) + 0.15 \cdot \left(\frac{j}{70}\right)^{10} \cdot \cos\left(f\left(\frac{i}{140}\right) \cdot 2 \cdot \pi\right)^3 + \alpha_{i,j}$$

$$\Theta_{i,j} := 0.35 \cdot \sin\left(f\left(\frac{i}{140}\right) \cdot 2 \cdot \pi\right) + 0.15 \cdot \frac{j}{70} \cdot \sin\left(f\left(\frac{i}{140}\right) \cdot 2 \cdot \pi\right) + \beta_{i,j}$$

$$K_{i,j} := \left(0.4 + 0.3 \cdot \cos\left(f\left(\frac{i}{140}\right) \cdot 2 \cdot \pi\right)\right) \cdot \sin\left(\frac{j}{70} \cdot \pi\right) + \gamma_{i,j}$$

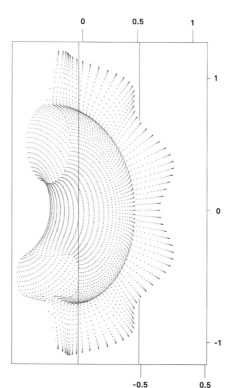

$(\Pi, \Theta, K)$

$\Theta_{i,0}$

$\Theta_{i,50}$

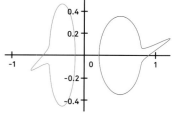

$\Pi_{i,0}, \Pi_{i,50}$

$K_{0,j}$

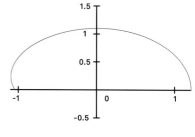

$\Pi_{0,j}$

Length: 36 mm | Width: 15 mm
Diameter: 8 mm
Cooking Time: 9 min

# GARGANELLI

A grooved *pasta corta* (short pasta), similar to *maccheroni* (see page 110) but with pointed slanting ends, *garganelli* are shaped like the gullet of a chicken ('*garganel*' in the northern Italian Emiliano-Romagnolo dialect). Traditionally cooked in broth, *garganelli* are also sometimes served in hare sauce with chopped bacon.

> STRAIGHT LONGITUDINAL PROFILE
> ⌄ HOLLOW CROSS-SECTION
> ⌄ STRIATED SURFACE
> ⌄ SMOOTH EDGES

_ranges

$i := 0, 1 .. 50$

$j := 0, 1 .. 150$

_equations

$$\alpha_{i,j} := \left(\frac{i-25}{125}\right) \cdot j \qquad \beta_{i,j} := \left(\frac{i-25}{125}\right) \cdot (150 - j)$$

$$\eta_{i,j} := \text{if}\left(j \le 75 \wedge i \le 25, \alpha_{i,j}, \text{if}\left(j \ge 75 \wedge i \le 25, \beta_{i,j}, \text{if}\left(j \ge 75 \wedge i \ge 25, \beta_{i,j}, \alpha_{i,j}\right)\right)\right)$$

$$\Pi_{i,j} := 0.1 \cdot \cos\left(\frac{j}{3} \cdot \pi\right) + \left(3 + \sin\left(\frac{\eta_{i,j}}{60} \cdot \pi\right)\right) \cdot \cos\left(\frac{7 \cdot \eta_{i,j}}{60} \cdot \pi\right)$$

$$\Theta_{i,j} := 0.1 \cdot \sin\left(\frac{j}{3} \cdot \pi\right) + \left(3 + \sin\left(\frac{\eta_{i,j}}{60} \cdot \pi\right)\right) \cdot \sin\left(\frac{7 \cdot \eta_{i,j}}{60} \cdot \pi\right)$$

$$K_{i,j} := \frac{6 \cdot j}{25} + \frac{\eta_{i,j}}{4}$$

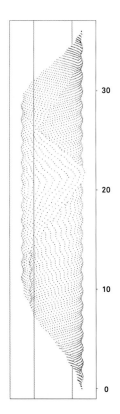

$(\Pi, \Theta, K)$

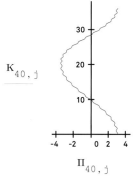

$K_{40,j}$

$\Pi_{40,j}$

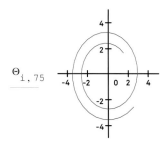

$\Theta_{i,75}$

$\Pi_{i,75}$

Length: 36 mm | Width: 9 mm
Cooking Time: 10 min

# GEMELLI

To create a *gemello*, a single pasta strand is twisted into a spiral with a deceptively dual appearance. In the south of Italy *gemelli* (twins) are served with tomato, mozzarella and basil, while in the northwest they are preferred with pesto and green beans, or in salads.

> TWISTED LONGITUDINAL PROFILE
>> SOLID CROSS-SECTION
>>> SMOOTH SURFACE
>>>> SMOOTH EDGES

_ranges

$i := 0, 1 .. \ 100$

$j := 0, 1 .. \ 50$

_equations

$$\Pi_{i,j} := 6 \cdot \cos\left(\frac{j}{50} \cdot 1.9\pi + 0.55 \cdot \pi\right) \cdot \cos\left(\frac{3 \cdot i}{25}\right)$$

$$\Theta_{i,j} := 6 \cdot \cos\left(\frac{j}{50} \cdot 1.9\pi + 0.55 \cdot \pi\right) \cdot \sin\left(\frac{3 \cdot i}{25}\right)$$

$$K_{i,j} := 8 \cdot \sin\left(\frac{j}{50} \cdot 1.9 \cdot \pi + 0.55 \cdot \pi\right) + \frac{3 \cdot i}{4}$$

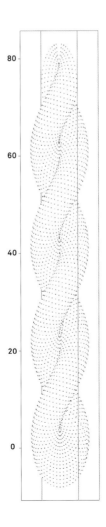

$(\Pi, \Theta, K)$

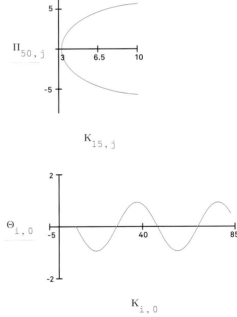

$\Pi_{50,j}$

$K_{15,j}$

$\Theta_{i,0}$

$K_{i,0}$

Length: 38 mm | Width: 6 mm
Cooking Time: 7 min

# GIGLI

With their fluted edges and cone-like shape, *gigli* resemble small bells (*campanelle*) or lilies (*gigli*), after which they are named. Another more recent design, *gigli* are shaped to capture thick meaty sauces.

> HELICOIDAL LONGITUDINAL PROFILE
>
> ∨ HOLLOW CROSS-SECTION
>
> ∨ SMOOTH SURFACE
>
> ∨ SMOOTH EDGES

_ranges

$i := 0, 1 .. \ 150$

$j := 0, 1 .. \ 40$

_equations

$$\Pi_{i,j} := \left(0.8 - 0.6 \cdot \sin\left(\frac{j}{80} \cdot \pi\right)^{0.5}\right) \cdot \cos\left(\frac{i}{50} \cdot \pi\right) + 0.08 \cdot \sin\left(\frac{j}{40} \cdot \pi\right)$$

$$\Theta_{i,j} := \left(0.8 - 0.6 \cdot \sin\left(\frac{j}{80} \cdot \pi\right)^{0.5}\right) \cdot \sin\left(\frac{i}{50} \cdot \pi\right) + 0.08 \cdot \sin\left(\frac{j}{40} \cdot \pi\right)$$

$$K_{i,j} := 1.1 \cdot \frac{j}{40} + 0.7 \cdot \left(1 - \sin\left(\frac{150 - i}{300} \cdot \pi\right)\right)^2$$

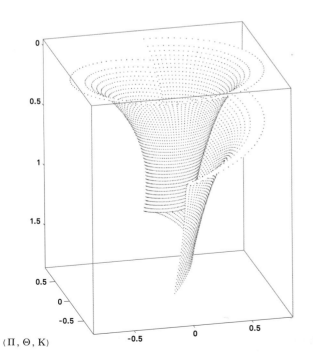

$(\Pi, \Theta, K)$

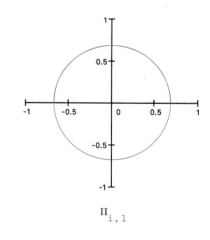

$\Theta_{i,1}$

$\Pi_{i,1}$

Length: 29 mm | Width: 10 mm
Cooking Time: 5–7 min

# GIGLIO ONDULATO

Identical to *gigli* but with crenellated edges, *giglio ondulato* are made of durum-wheat flour and water.

> HELICOIDAL LONGITUDINAL PROFILE
ᵥ HOLLOW CROSS-SECTION
ᵥ SMOOTH SURFACE
ᵥ CRENELLATED EDGES

_ranges

$i := 0, 1 .. \ 150$

$j := 0, 1 .. \ 40$

_equations

$$\alpha_{i,j} := 0.6 + 0.03 \cdot \left(\frac{40-j}{40}\right)^{10} \cdot \cos\left(\frac{4 \cdot i + 75}{15} \cdot \pi\right) - 0.5 \cdot \sin\left(\frac{j}{80} \cdot \pi\right)^{0.6}$$

$$\beta_{i,j} := \sin\left(\frac{2 \cdot i}{75} \cdot \pi\right) + \left(\frac{i}{150}\right)^{10} \cdot \left(0.08 \cdot \sin\left(\frac{j}{40} \cdot \pi\right) + 0.03 \cdot \sin\left(\frac{j}{5} \cdot \pi\right)\right)$$

$$\Pi_{i,j} := \alpha_{i,j} \cdot \cos\left(\frac{2 \cdot i}{75} \cdot \pi\right) + \left(\frac{i}{150}\right)^{10} \cdot \left(0.08 \sin\left(\frac{j}{40} \cdot \pi\right) + 0.03 \cdot \cos\left(\frac{j}{5} \cdot \pi\right)\right)$$

$$\Theta_{i,j} := \left[0.6 + 0.03 \cdot \left(\frac{40-j}{40}\right)^{10} \cdot \sin\left(\frac{4 \cdot i}{15} \cdot \pi\right) - 0.5 \cdot \sin\left(\frac{j}{80} \cdot \pi\right)^{0.6}\right] \cdot \beta_{i,j}$$

$$K_{i,j} := 1.1 \cdot \frac{j}{40} + 0.7 \cdot \left(1 - \sin\left(\frac{150-i}{300} \cdot \pi\right)\right)$$

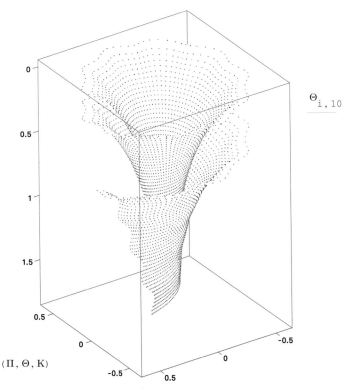

$(\Pi, \Theta, K)$

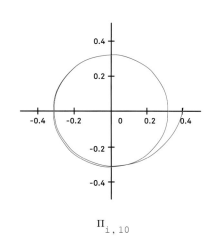

$\Theta_{i, 10}$

$\Pi_{i, 10}$

Length: 30 mm | Width: 15 mm
Cooking Time: 7–8 min

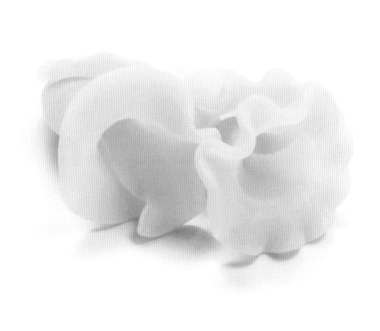

# GNOCCHETTI SARDI

As their name suggests, *gnocchetti* are simply small *gnocchi* (or 'dumplings'). They go well with ricotta or Pecorino Romano cheese, or served with thick sauces such as a veal *ragù*. *Gnocchetti* originated in Sardinia, a Mediterranean island to the west of Italy.

> PINCHED LONGITUDINAL PROFILE
⌄ SEMI-OPEN CROSS-SECTION
⌄ STRIATED SURFACE
⌄ SMOOTH EDGES

_ranges

$i := 0, 1 .. 50$

$j := 0, 1 .. 150$

_equations

$$\alpha_j := 0.8 + 3 \cdot \sin\left(\frac{j}{150} \cdot \pi\right)^{0.8} \qquad \beta_{i,j} := \left| \cos\left(\frac{2 \cdot j + 7.5}{15} \cdot \pi\right) \right|$$

$$\Pi_{i,j} := \alpha_j \cdot \cos\left(\frac{i}{50} \cdot \pi\right) + 0.2 \cdot \cos\left(\frac{i}{50} \cdot \pi\right) \cdot \sin\left(\frac{j}{150} \cdot \pi\right) \cdot \beta_{i,j}$$

$$\Theta_{i,j} := \alpha_j \cdot \sin\left(\frac{i}{50} \cdot \pi\right) + 0.2 \cdot \sin\left(\frac{i}{50} \cdot \pi\right) \cdot \sin\left(\frac{j}{150} \cdot \pi\right) \cdot \beta_{i,j}$$

$$K_{i,j} := 13 \cdot \cos\left(\frac{j}{150} \cdot \pi\right)$$

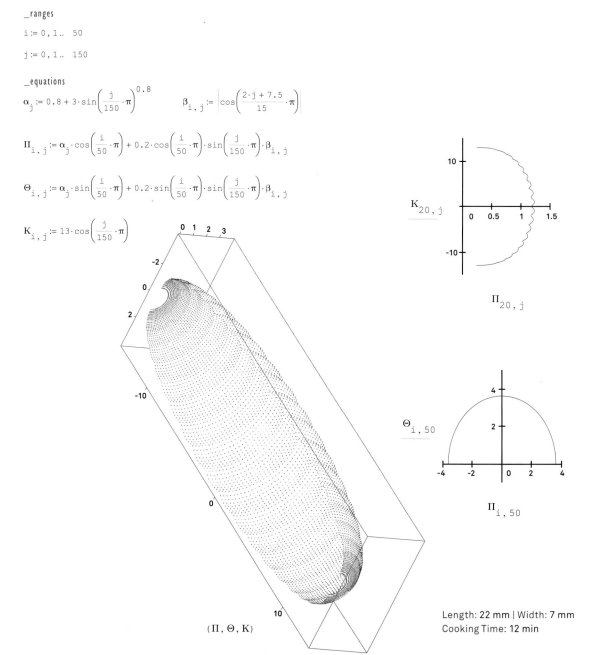

$\dfrac{K_{20,j}}{\Pi_{20,j}}$

$\dfrac{\Theta_{i,50}}{\Pi_{i,50}}$

$(\Pi, \Theta, K)$

Length: 22 mm | Width: 7 mm
Cooking Time: 12 min

# GNOCCHI

Members of an extended family, *gnocchi* (dumplings) often resemble a semi-open grooved shell. Their preparation and ingredients (including potato, durum wheat, buckwheat and semolina) vary according to type. *Gnocchi* are often added to a sauce made from fontina cheese.

> PINCHED LONGITUDINAL PROFILE

∨ SEMI-OPEN CROSS-SECTION

∨ STRIATED SURFACE

∨ SMOOTH EDGES

_ranges

$i := 0, 1 .. \ 40$

$j := 0, 1 .. \ 130$

_equations

$$\alpha_{i,j} := \frac{i}{40} \cdot \sin\left(\frac{j}{130} \cdot \pi\right) \qquad \beta_{i,j} := \left| \cos\left(\frac{j+13}{26} \cdot \pi\right) \right|$$

$$\Pi_{i,j} := 0.2 \cdot \cos\left(\frac{i}{40} \cdot 1.3 \cdot \pi\right) \cdot \sin\left(\frac{j}{130} \cdot \pi\right) \cdot \beta_{i,j} + \alpha_{i,j} \cdot \cos\left(\frac{i}{40} \cdot 1.3 \cdot \pi\right)$$

$$\Theta_{i,j} := 0.2 \cdot \sin\left(\frac{i}{40} \cdot 1.3 \cdot \pi\right) \cdot \sin\left(\frac{j}{130} \cdot \pi\right) \cdot \beta_{i,j} + \alpha_{i,j} \cdot \sin\left(\frac{i}{40} \cdot 1.3 \cdot \pi\right)$$

$$K_{i,j} := 1.5 \cdot \cos\left(\frac{j}{130} \pi\right)$$

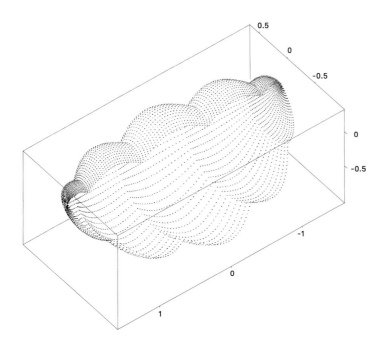

$(\Pi, \Theta, K)$

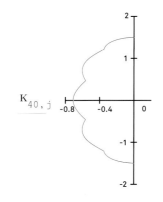

$K_{40,j}$

$\Pi_{40,j}$

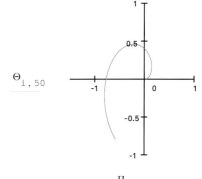

$\Theta_{i,50}$

$\Pi_{i,50}$

Length: 32 mm | Width: 16 mm
Cooking Time: 10 min

# GRAMIGNA

A speciality of the northern Italian region of Emilia-Romagna, *gramigna* (little weed) are traditionally served with a chunky sauce of sausages, or accompanied by the world-famous *ragù alla bolognese*. Alternatively, *gramigna* are sometimes presented *alla pomodoro* (with a light tomato sauce).

&gt; BENT LONGITUDINAL PROFILE

⌄ HOLLOW CROSS-SECTION

⌄ SMOOTH SURFACE

⌄ SMOOTH EDGES

_ranges

$i := 0, 1 .. \ 25$

$j := 0, 1 .. \ 150$

_equations

$$\Pi_{i,j} := \left[ 0.5 + 5.6 \cdot \left( \frac{j}{150} \right)^2 + 0.3 \cdot \cos \left( \frac{2 \cdot i}{25} \cdot \pi \right) \right] \cdot \cos \left( \frac{2.1 \cdot j}{150} \cdot \pi \right)$$

$$\Theta_{i,j} := 0.3 \cdot \sin \left( \frac{2 \cdot i}{25} \cdot \pi \right)$$

$$K_{i,j} := \left[ 0.5 + 3.2 \left( \frac{j}{150} \right)^2 + 0.3 \cdot \cos \left( \frac{2 \cdot i}{25} \cdot \pi \right) \right] \cdot \sin \left( \frac{2.1 \cdot j}{150} \cdot \pi \right)$$

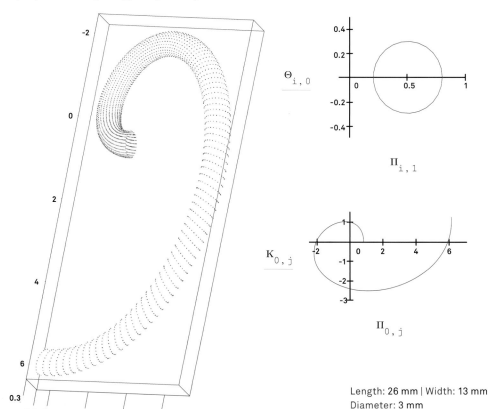

$(\Pi, \Theta, K)$

$\Theta_{i,0}$

$\Pi_{i,1}$

$K_{0,j}$

$\Pi_{0,j}$

Length: 26 mm | Width: 13 mm
Diameter: 3 mm
Cooking Time: 9 min

# LANCETTE

No longer than 15 mm, *lancette* or 'hands' (of a clock) belong to the *pastine minute* (tiny pasta) clan. They are delicious in consommés with a sprinkling of croutons and chopped greens. *Lancette* are also an excellent addition to mushroom or chicken soups.

> PINCHED LONGITUDINAL PROFILE

⌄ SOLID CROSS-SECTION

⌄ SMOOTH SURFACE

⌄ SMOOTH EDGES

_ranges

$i := 0, 1 .. 50$

$j := 0, 1 .. 90$

_equations

$$\alpha_{i,j} := 0.4 \cdot \sin\left(\frac{5 \cdot j}{9} \cdot \pi\right) \qquad \beta_{i,j} := \sin\left(\frac{j + 45}{90} \cdot \pi\right)$$

$$\gamma_{i,j} := \left(\frac{3 \cdot i - 75}{5}\right) \cdot \sin\left(\frac{j}{90} \cdot \pi\right) - \left(1 - \sin\left(\frac{i}{50} \cdot \pi\right)\right)^{25} \cdot \alpha_{i,j} \cdot \beta_{i,j}$$

$$\zeta_{i,j} := \text{if}\left(i \le 25, \gamma_{i,j}, 30 \cdot \frac{i - 25}{50} \cdot \sin\left(\frac{j}{90} \cdot \pi\right) + \sin\left(\frac{i - 25}{50} \cdot \pi\right) \cdot \alpha_{i,j} \cdot \beta_{i,j}\right)$$

$$\Pi_{i,j} := 4 \cdot \cos\left(\frac{3 \cdot \zeta_{i,j}}{50} \cdot \pi\right)$$

$$\Theta_{i,j} := 4 \cdot \sin\left(\frac{3 \cdot \zeta_{i,j}}{50} \cdot \pi\right) \cdot \left[0.3 + \left(1 - \sin\left(\frac{j}{90} \cdot \pi\right)\right)^{0.6}\right]$$

$$K_{i,j} := \frac{j}{3}$$

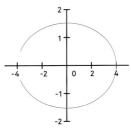

$\Theta_{i, 50}$

$\Pi_{i, 50}$

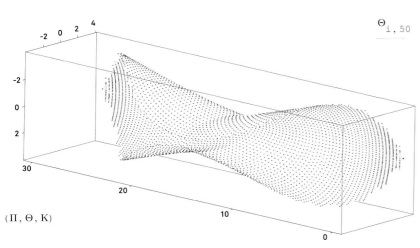

$(\Pi, \Theta, K)$

Length: **15 mm** | Width: **5 mm**
Cooking Time: **6 min**

# LASAGNA LARGA DOPPIA RICCIA

As their name suggests, *lasagna larga doppia riccia* (large doubly curled *lasagna*) have two long undulating edges. The curls give the pasta a variable consistency when cooked, and help them to collect sauce. *Lasagne* are excellent with ricotta and a *ragù napoletano*, or cooked *al forno* (at the oven) with a creamy *besciamella* sauce.

> STRAIGHT LONGITUDINAL PROFILE
> ⌄ SOLID CROSS-SECTION
> ⌄ SMOOTH SURFACE
> ⌄ CRENELLATED EDGES

_ranges

$i := 0, 1 .. 50$

$j := 0, 1 .. 150$

_equations

$$\Pi_{i,j} := if\left[8 \leq i \leq 42, \frac{5}{6} + \frac{5 \cdot i - 40}{34}, if\left[i \leq 8, \frac{5 \cdot i}{48}, \frac{5}{6} \cdot \left(7 + \frac{i - 42}{8}\right)\right]\right]$$

$$\Theta_{i,j} := \frac{j}{15}$$

$$K_{i,j} := if\left[8 \leq i \leq 42, 0, if\left[i \leq 8, \frac{8 - i}{32} \cdot \cos\left(\frac{j + 3}{6} \cdot \pi\right), 0.25 \cdot \left(\frac{i - 42}{8}\right) \cdot \cos\left(\frac{j + 9}{6} \cdot \pi\right)\right]\right]$$

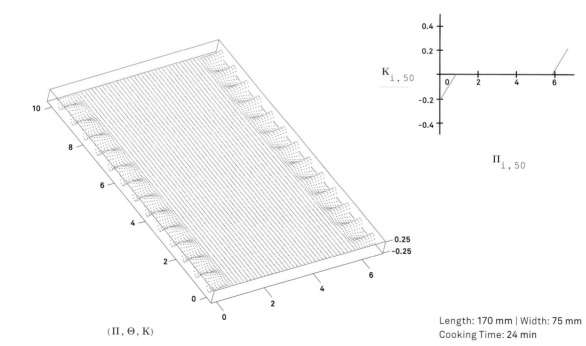

$(\Pi, \Theta, K)$

Length: 170 mm | Width: 75 mm
Cooking Time: 24 min

# LINGUINE

The thinnest member of the *bavette* (little dribble) family, *linguine* (little tongues) are best accompanied by fresh tomato, herbs, a drop of olive oil, garlic, anchovies and hot peppers. *Linguine* may also be served with shellfish sauces, or white sauces of cream and soft cheese, flavoured with lemon, saffron or ginger.

> STRAIGHT LONGITUDINAL PROFILE
> ⌄ SOLID CROSS-SECTION
> ⌄ SMOOTH SURFACE
> ⌄ SMOOTH EDGES

_ranges

$i := 0, 1 .. 150$

$j := 0, 1 .. 50$

_equations

$$\Pi_{i,j} := \cos\left(\frac{i}{75} \cdot \pi\right)$$

$$\Theta_{i,j} := 2 \cdot \sin\left(\frac{i}{75} \cdot \pi\right)$$

$$K_{i,j} := \frac{j}{5}$$

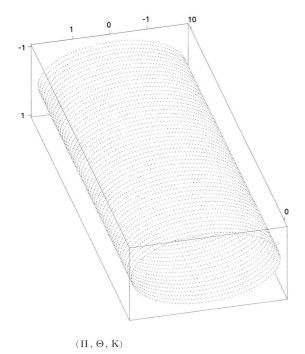

$(\Pi, \Theta, K)$

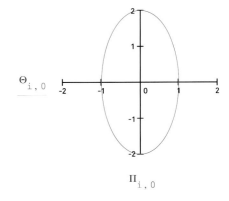

$\Theta_{i,0}$

$\Pi_{i,0}$

Length: 255 mm | Width: 3 mm
Cooking Time: 11 min

# LUMACONI RIGATI

Originally from Campania and Liguria, *lumaconi rigati* (big ribbed snails) can be stuffed with a wide range of fillings, including spinach and ricotta cheese. Like cannelloni (page 027), they can then be covered in *besciamella* and cooked in the oven. Smaller members of the family (*lumache*) are also available.

> BENT LONGITUDINAL PROFILE

∨ HOLLOW CROSS-SECTION

∨ STRIATED SURFACE

∨ SMOOTH EDGES

_ranges

$i := 0, 1 .. \ 240$

$j := 0, 1 .. \ 60$

_equations

$$\alpha_{i,j} := 0.45 + 0.01 \cdot \cos\left(\frac{i}{3} \cdot \pi\right) + \frac{j}{300} \cdot \left|\cos\left(\frac{i}{240} \cdot \pi\right)\right| \cdot \cos\left(\frac{i}{120} \cdot \pi\right)^{20}$$

$$\beta_{i,j} := \frac{j}{300} \cdot \left|\cos\left(\frac{i}{240} \cdot \pi\right)\right| \sin\left(\frac{i}{120} \cdot \pi\right) + 0.125 \cdot \left(\frac{j}{60}\right)^{6} \cdot \sin\left(\frac{i}{120} \cdot \pi\right)$$

$$\Pi_{i,j} := \left(0.4 \cdot \cos\left(\frac{i}{120} \cdot \pi\right) + \alpha_{i,j}\right) \cdot \cos\left(\frac{j}{60} \cdot \pi\right) + 0.48 \cdot \left(\frac{j}{60}\right)^{6} \cdot \sin\left(\frac{i+60}{120} \cdot \pi\right)^{3}$$

$$\Theta_{i,j} := 0.5 \cdot \sin\left(\frac{i}{120} \cdot \pi\right) + 0.01 \cdot \sin\left(\frac{i}{3} \cdot \pi\right) + \beta_{i,j}$$

$$K_{i,j} := \left(0.45 + 0.4 \cdot \cos\left(\frac{i}{120} \cdot \pi\right)\right) \cdot \sin\left(\frac{j}{60} \cdot \pi\right)$$

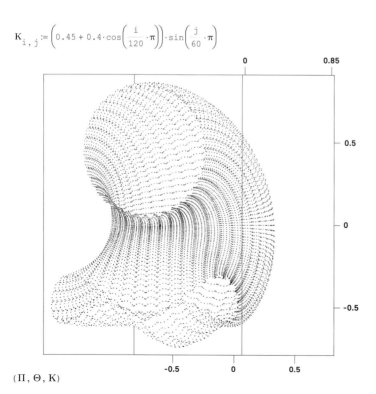

$(\Pi, \Theta, K)$

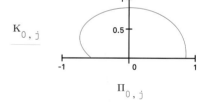

$$\frac{K_{0,j}}{\Pi_{0,j}}$$

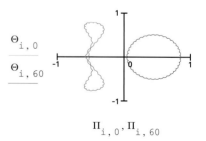

$$\frac{\Theta_{i,0}}{\Theta_{i,60}}$$

$$\Pi_{i,0}, \Pi_{i,60}$$

Length: 47 mm | Width: 38 mm
Cooking Time: 13 min

# MACCHERONI

The origin of the name *maccheroni* is uncertain. It is used generically to describe a hollow *pasta corta* (short pasta) that is made of durum-wheat flour and perhaps eggs. The pasta can be served *con le sarde* (with sardines) – a dish enhanced by a touch of fennel.

> STRAIGHT LONGITUDINAL PROFILE
> ∨ HOLLOW CROSS-SECTION
> ∨ STRIATED SURFACE
> ∨ SMOOTH EDGES

_ranges

$i := 0, 1 .. \ 150$

$j := 0, 1 .. \ 50$

_equations

$$\Pi_{i,j} := 8 \cdot \cos\left(\frac{i}{75} \cdot \pi\right) + 0.2 \cdot \cos\left(\frac{4 \cdot i}{15} \cdot \pi\right) + 5 \cdot \cos\left(\frac{j}{100} \cdot \pi\right)$$

$$\Theta_{i,j} := 8 \cdot \sin\left(\frac{i}{75} \cdot \pi\right) + 0.2 \cdot \sin\left(\frac{4 \cdot i}{15} \cdot \pi\right) + 4 \cdot \sin\left(\frac{j}{100} \cdot \pi\right)$$

$$K_{i,j} := \frac{6 \cdot j}{5}$$

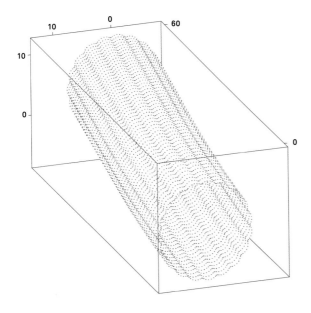

$(\Pi, \Theta, K)$

$\Theta_{i,1}$

$\Pi_{i,1}$

Diameter: 8 mm | Length: 40 mm
Cooking Time: 12 min

# MACCHERONI ALLA CHITARRA

Coming from the central Italian region of Abruzzo, *maccheroni alla chitarra* (guitar *maccheroni*) have a square cross-section, produced when a thin sheet of pasta is pressed through a frame of closely ranged wires (or *chitarra*) that lends the pasta its name. Usually served with a mutton *ragù*, or *pallottelle* (veal meatballs).

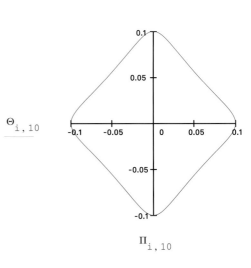

> STRAIGHT LONGITUDINAL PROFILE

∨ SOLID CROSS-SECTION

∨ SMOOTH SURFACE

∨ SMOOTH EDGES

_ranges

$i := 0, 1 .. 120$

$j := 0, 1 .. 60$

_equations

$$\Pi_{i,j} := 0.05 \cdot \cos\left(\frac{i}{60} \cdot \pi\right)^3 + 0.05 \cdot \cos\left(\frac{i}{60} \cdot \pi\right)$$

$$\Theta_{i,j} := 0.05 \cdot \sin\left(\frac{i}{60} \cdot \pi\right)^3 + 0.05 \cdot \sin\left(\frac{i}{60} \cdot \pi\right)$$

$$K_{i,j} := \frac{j}{60}$$

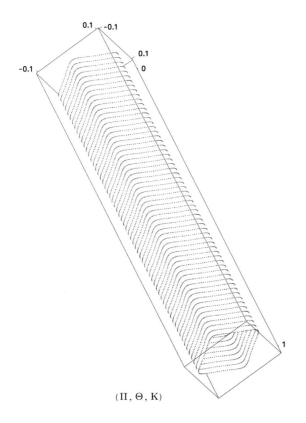

$(\Pi, \Theta, K)$

$\Theta_{i, 10}$

$\Pi_{i, 10}$

Length: 258 mm | Width: 2 mm
Cooking Time: 11 min

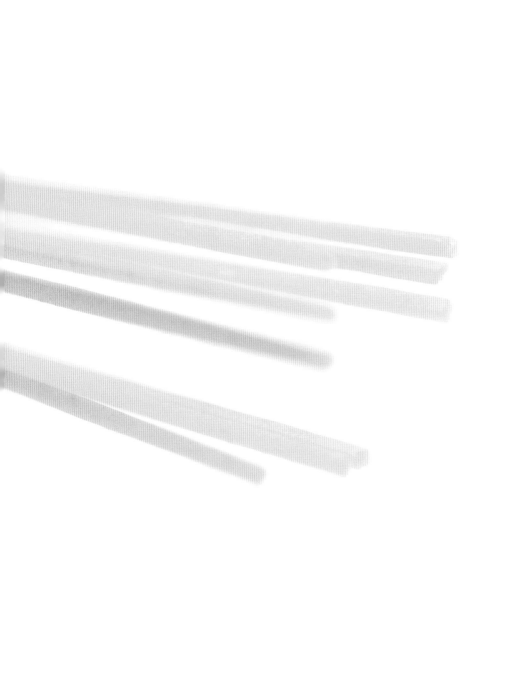

# MAFALDINE

Named at the turn of the twentieth century after Princess Mafalda of the House of Savoy, *mafaldine* are thin flat sheets of durum-wheat flour pasta with a rippled finish on each long edge. They are generally served with meaty sauces such as *ragù napoletano* or in seafood dishes.

> STRAIGHT LONGITUDINAL PROFILE
⌄ SOLID CROSS-SECTION
⌄ SMOOTH SURFACE
⌄ CRENELLATED EDGES

_ranges

$i := 0, 1 .. 30$

$j := 0, 1 .. 150$

_equations

$$\Pi_{i,j} := \frac{7 \cdot i}{18}$$

$$\Theta_{i,j} := \frac{j}{3}$$

$$K_{i,j} := \text{if}\left[6 \leq i \leq 24, 0, \text{if}\left[i \leq 6, \left(\frac{6-i}{6}\right) \cdot \cos\left(\frac{j+5}{10} \cdot \pi\right), \left(\frac{i-24}{6}\right) \cdot \cos\left(\frac{j+15}{10} \cdot \pi\right)\right]\right]$$

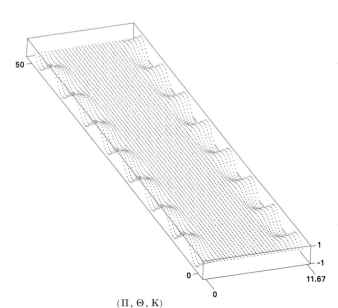

$(\Pi, \Theta, K)$

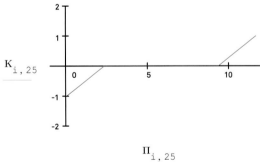

$K_{i, 25}$

$\Pi_{i, 25}$

Length: 240 mm | Width: 13 mm
Cooking Time: 9 min

# MANICOTTI

One of the oldest-known durum-wheat varieties, *manicotti* (sleeves) were originally prepared by cutting dough into rectangles, which were topped with stuffing, rolled and finally baked *al forno* (at the oven). Today they are served containing a variety of cheeses and covered in a savoury sauce, like filled dinner crêpes.

> SHEARED LONGITUDINAL PROFILE
> ⌄ HOLLOW CROSS-SECTION
> ⌄ STRIATED SURFACE
> ⌄ SMOOTH EDGES

_ranges

$i := 0, 1 .. \ 200$

$j := 0, 1 .. \ 40$

_equations

$$\alpha_{i,j} := -7 \cdot \sin\left(\frac{i-100}{100} \cdot \pi\right)^2 + 0.3 \cdot \sin\left(\frac{3 \cdot i - 300}{10} \cdot \pi\right)$$

$$\beta_{i,j} := -8 \cdot \cos\left(\frac{i-100}{100} \cdot \pi\right) + 0.3 \cdot \cos\left(\frac{3 \cdot i - 300}{10} \cdot \pi\right)$$

$$\gamma_{i,j} := -8 \cdot \cos\left(\frac{i-100}{100} \cdot \pi\right) + 22 \cdot \sin\left(\frac{j-20}{40} \cdot \pi\right)$$

$$\Pi_{i,j} := if\left(i < 100, 7 \cdot \sin\left(\frac{i}{100} \cdot \pi\right)^2 + 0.3 \cdot \sin\left(\frac{3 \cdot i}{10} \cdot \pi\right), \alpha_{i,j}\right)$$

$$\Theta_{i,j} := if\left(i < 100, 8 \cdot \cos\left(\frac{i}{100} \cdot \pi\right) + 0.3 \cdot \cos\left(\frac{3 \cdot i}{10} \cdot \pi\right), \beta_{i,j}\right)$$

$$K_{i,j} := if\left(i < 100, 8 \cdot \cos\left(\frac{i}{100} \cdot \pi\right) + 22 \cdot \sin\left(\frac{j-20}{40}\pi\right), \gamma_{i,j}\right)$$

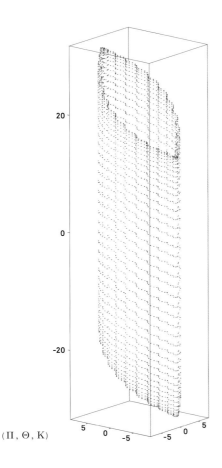

$(\Pi, \Theta, K)$

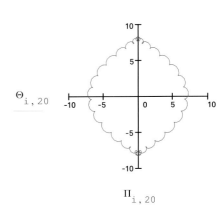

$\Theta_{i,20}$

$\Pi_{i,20}$

Length: 130 mm | Width: 35 mm
Cooking Time: 8 min

# ORECCHIETTE

This pasta is popular in the southeastern coastal region of Puglia in Italy, where it is customarily cooked in dishes with rapini, a relative of broccoli that grows plentifully in the area. *Orecchiette* (little ears) also pair well with other vegetables such as beans, and with salty seasonings such as anchovies, capers or olives.

> STRAIGHT LONGITUDINAL PROFILE
> ⌄ SEMI-OPEN CROSS-SECTION
> ⌄ STRIATED SURFACE
> ⌄ CRENELLATED EDGES

_ranges

$i := 0, 1 .. 150$

$j := 0, 1 .. 15$

_equations

$$\Pi_{i,j} := \frac{2 \cdot j}{3} \cdot \cos\left(\frac{i}{75} \cdot \pi\right) + 0.3 \cdot \cos\left(\frac{2 \cdot i}{15} \cdot \pi\right)$$

$$\Theta_{i,j} := 10 \cdot \sin\left(\frac{i}{75} \cdot \pi\right)$$

$$K_{i,j} := 0.1 \cdot \cos\left(\frac{i}{3} \cdot \pi\right) + 5 \cdot \left(0.5 + 0.5 \cdot \cos\left(\frac{2 \cdot i}{75} \cdot \pi\right)\right)^4 \cdot \cos\left(\frac{j}{30} \cdot \pi\right)^2 + 1.5 \cdot \left(0.5 + 0.5 \cdot \cos\left(\frac{2 \cdot i}{75} \cdot \pi\right)\right)^5 \cdot \sin\left(\frac{j}{30} \cdot \pi\right)^{10}$$

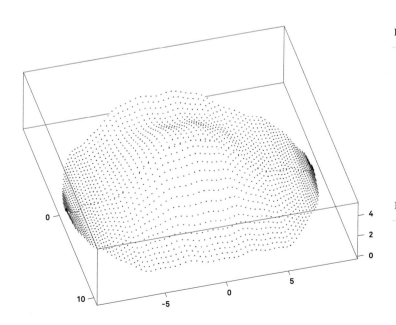

$(\Pi, \Theta, K)$

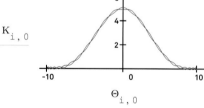

$\dfrac{K_{i,0}}{\Theta_{i,0}}$

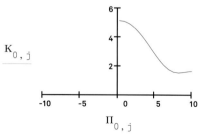

$\dfrac{K_{0,j}}{\Pi_{0,j}}$

Width: 7 mm | Diameter: 20 mm
Cooking Time: 11 min

# PACCHERI

Part of the *pasta corta* (short pasta) family, *paccheri* are ribbed pasta cylinders that (due to their large size) are recommended with aubergine, seafood or indeed any chunky sauce. It is thought the name stems from the term *paccare*, which means 'to smack' in the southern Italian region of Campania.

> STRAIGHT LONGITUDINAL PROFILE
> ∨ HOLLOW CROSS-SECTION
> ∨ SMOOTH SURFACE
> ∨ SMOOTH EDGES

_ranges

$i := 0, 1 .. \ 150$

$j := 0, 1 .. \ 30$

_equations

$$\Pi_{i,j} := \left(\frac{j+60}{60}\right) \cdot \cos\left(\frac{i}{75} \cdot \pi\right) + 0.5 \cdot \cos\left(\frac{j}{60} \cdot \pi\right) + \cos\left(\frac{i+j}{75} \cdot \pi\right)$$

$$\Theta_{i,j} := 2.6 \cdot \sin\left(\frac{i}{75} \cdot \pi\right) + 0.3 \cdot \sin\left(\frac{j}{60} \cdot \pi\right)$$

$$K_{i,j} := \frac{7 \cdot j}{30}$$

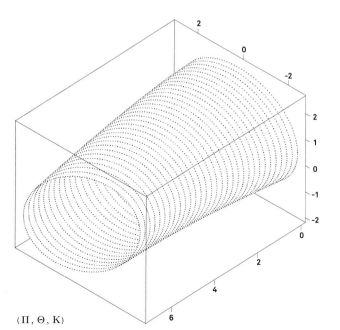

$(\Pi, \Theta, K)$

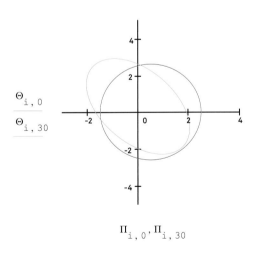

$\Theta_{i,0}$
$\Theta_{i,30}$

$\Pi_{i,0}, \Pi_{i,30}$

Length: **46 mm** | Width: **29 mm**
Cooking Time: **12 min**

# PAPPARDELLE

This *pasta lunga* (long pasta) is often cooked with duck, pigeon or other game fowl. *Pappardelle* are so popular that towns in Italy hold festivals in their honour, such as the *Sagra delle Pappardelle al Cinghiale* (Feast of the *Pappardelle* and Boar) in Torre Alfina, central Italy.

> BENT LONGITUDINAL PROFILE
⌄ SOLID CROSS-SECTION
⌄ SMOOTH SURFACE
⌄ SMOOTH EDGES

_ranges

$i := 0, 1 .. 800$

$j := 0, 1 .. 5$

_equations

$$\Pi_{i,j} := \cos\left(\frac{i}{80} \cdot \pi\right) + \frac{3 \cdot j}{50} \cdot \sin\left(\frac{21 \cdot i}{800} \cdot \pi\right)$$

$$\Theta_{i,j} := \sin\left(\frac{i}{3200} \cdot \pi\right)^{0.1} \cdot \sin\left(\frac{i}{80} \cdot \pi\right)$$

$$K_{i,j} := \frac{3 \cdot j}{50} + 0.5 \cdot \sin\left(\frac{i}{200} \cdot \pi\right)$$

$$T_{i,j} := \cos\left(\frac{i}{80} \cdot \pi\right) + \frac{3 \cdot j}{50} \cdot \sin\left(\frac{21 \cdot i}{800} \cdot \pi\right)$$

$$X_{i,j} := \sin\left(\frac{i}{3200} \cdot \pi\right)^{0.5} \cdot \sin\left(\frac{i}{80} \cdot \pi\right)$$

$$\Psi_{i,j} := \frac{3 \cdot j}{50} + 0.5 \cdot \sin\left(\frac{i}{200} \cdot \pi\right)$$

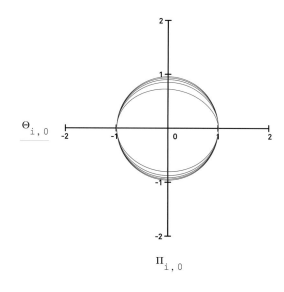

$\underline{\Theta_{i,0}}$

$\Pi_{i,0}$

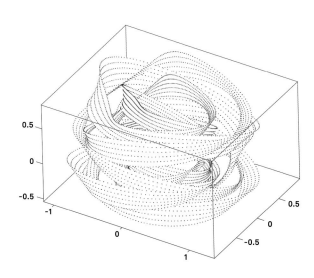

$(\Pi, \Theta, K) , (0.6T, 0.8X, 0.9\Psi)$

Width: **18 mm** | Diameter: **50 mm**
Cooking Time: **7 min**

# PENNE RIGATE

A versatile pasta, *penne rigate* (grooved quills) come from Campania, in southern Italy, and belong to the *pasta corta* (short pasta) family. They can be served with spicy *arrabbiata* (angry) sauce, which gets its name from the chillies and red peppers it contains.

> SHEARED LONGITUDINAL PROFILE
> ⌄ HOLLOW CROSS-SECTION
> ⌄ STRIATED SURFACE
> ⌄ SMOOTH EDGES

_ranges

$i := 0, 1 .. \ 170$

$j := 0, 1 .. \ 40$

_equations

$$\Pi_{i,j} := \mathrm{if}\left[ i < 85, \ 4 \cdot \sin\left(\frac{i}{85} \cdot \pi\right)^2 + 0.1 \cdot \sin\left(\frac{6 \cdot i}{17} \cdot \pi\right), \ -4 \cdot \sin\left(\frac{i - 85}{85} \cdot \pi\right)^2 + 0.1 \cdot \sin\left[\frac{6 \cdot (i - 85)}{17} \cdot \pi\right]\right]$$

$$\Theta_{i,j} := \mathrm{if}\left[ i < 85, \ 4 \cdot \cos\left(\frac{i}{85} \cdot \pi\right) + 0.1 \cdot \cos\left(\frac{6 \cdot i}{17} \cdot \pi\right), \ -4 \cdot \cos\left(\frac{i - 85}{85} \cdot \pi\right) + 0.1 \cdot \cos\left[\frac{6 \cdot (i - 85)}{17} \cdot \pi\right]\right]$$

$$K_{i,j} := \mathrm{if}\left( i < 85, \ 7 \cdot \cos\left(\frac{i}{85} \cdot \pi\right) + 15 \cdot \sin\left(\frac{j - 20}{40} \pi\right), \ -7 \cdot \cos\left(\frac{i - 85}{85} \cdot \pi\right) + 15 \cdot \sin\left(\frac{j - 20}{40} \pi\right)\right)$$

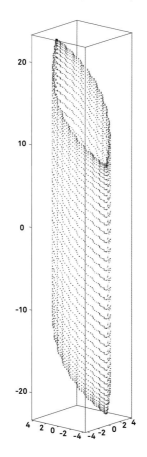

$(\Pi, \Theta, K)$

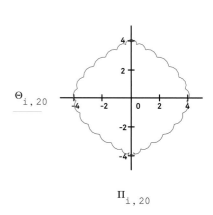

$\Theta_{i, 20}$

$\Pi_{i, 20}$

Length: 55 mm | Diameter: 8 mm
Cooking Time: 13 min

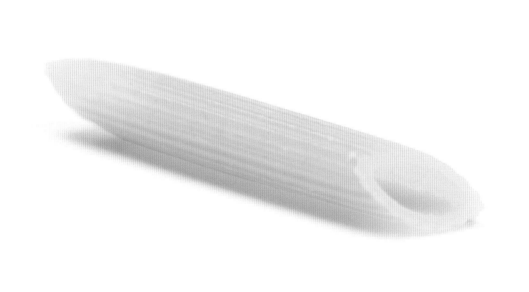

# PENNONI LISCI

Similar in appearance to *penne rigate*, but larger and without the grooves, *pennoni* (large quills) require a more oily sauce (perhaps containing sliced chorizo) to cling to their smooth surface.

› SHEARED LONGITUDINAL PROFILE
ᵥ HOLLOW CROSS-SECTION
ᵥ SMOOTH SURFACE
ᵥ SMOOTH EDGES

_ranges

$i := 0, 1 .. 200$

$j := 0, 1 .. 40$

_equations

$$\Pi_{i,j} := if\left(i < 100, 7 \cdot \sin\left(\frac{i}{100} \cdot \pi\right)^2, -7 \cdot \sin\left(\frac{i-100}{100} \cdot \pi\right)^2\right)$$

$$\Theta_{i,j} := if\left(i < 100, 8 \cdot \cos\left(\frac{i}{100} \cdot \pi\right), -8 \cdot \cos\left(\frac{i-100}{100} \cdot \pi\right)\right)$$

$$K_{i,j} := if\left(i < 100, 12 \cdot \cos\left(\frac{i}{100} \cdot \pi\right) + 15 \cdot \sin\left(\frac{j-20}{40} \cdot \pi\right), -12 \cdot \cos\left(\frac{i-100}{100} \cdot \pi\right) + 15 \cdot \sin\left(\frac{j-20}{40} \pi\right)\right)$$

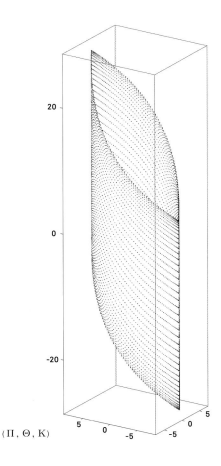

$(\Pi, \Theta, K)$

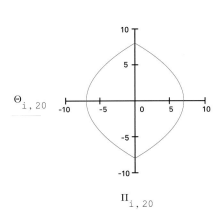

$\Theta_{i, 20}$

$\Pi_{i, 20}$

Length: 75 mm | Width: 28 mm
Cooking Time: 10 min

# PENNONI RIGATI

The angled trim of the *penne* pasta family makes its members easy
to recognize. *Pennoni rigati* (large grooved quills) are the ridged
version of *pennoni*, and can be stuffed and cooked.

› SHEARED LONGITUDINAL PROFILE

⌄ HOLLOW CROSS-SECTION

⌄ STRIATED SURFACE

⌄ SMOOTH EDGES

_ranges

$i := 0, 1 .. 200$

$j := 0, 1 .. 40$

_equations

$$\alpha_{i,j} := -7 \cdot \sin\left(\frac{i-100}{100} \cdot \pi\right)^2 + 0.2 \cdot \sin\left(\frac{3 \cdot i - 300}{10} \cdot \pi\right)$$

$$\Pi_{i,j} := \mathrm{if}\left(i < 100, \, 7 \cdot \sin\left(\frac{i}{100} \cdot \pi\right)^2 + 0.15 \cdot \sin\left(\frac{3 \cdot i}{10} \cdot \pi\right), \, \alpha_{i,j}\right)$$

$$\beta_{i,j} := -8 \cdot \cos\left(\frac{i-100}{100} \cdot \pi\right) + 0.2 \cdot \cos\left(\frac{3 \cdot i - 300}{10} \cdot \pi\right)$$

$$\Theta_{i,j} := \mathrm{if}\left(i < 100, \, 8 \cdot \cos\left(\frac{i}{100} \cdot \pi\right) + 0.15 \cdot \cos\left(\frac{3 \cdot i}{10} \cdot \pi\right), \, \beta_{i,j}\right)$$

$$\gamma_{i,j} := -12 \cdot \cos\left(\frac{i-100}{100} \cdot \pi\right) + 15 \cdot \sin\left(\frac{j-20}{40} \cdot \pi\right)$$

$$K_{i,j} := \mathrm{if}\left(i < 100, \, 12 \cdot \cos\left(\frac{i}{100} \cdot \pi\right) + 15 \cdot \sin\left(\frac{j-20}{40} \, \pi\right), \, \gamma_{i,j}\right)$$

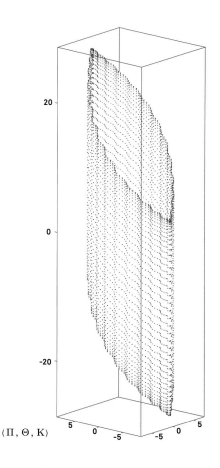

$(\Pi, \Theta, K)$

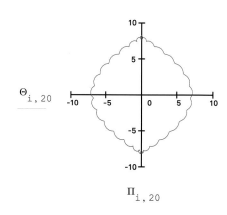

$\Theta_{i,20}$

$\Pi_{i,20}$

Length: **84 mm** | Width: **28 mm**
Cooking Time: **13 min**

# PUNTALETTE

Another member of the *pastine minute* (tiny pasta) family, *puntalette* (tiny tips) are about 9 mm long, and no thicker than 3 mm. Like most *pastine*, they are best consumed in creamy soups, or perhaps in salad.

> PINCHED LONGITUDINAL PROFILE
> ⌄ SOLID CROSS-SECTION
> ⌄ SMOOTH SURFACE
> ⌄ SMOOTH EDGES

_ranges

$i := 0, 1 .. 80$

$j := 0, 1 .. 80$

_equations

$$\Pi_{i,j} := 1.4 \cdot \sin\left(\frac{j}{80} \cdot \pi\right)^{1.2} \cdot \cos\left(\frac{i}{40} \cdot \pi\right)$$

$$\Theta_{i,j} := 2.5 \cdot \sin\left(\frac{j}{80} \cdot \pi\right)^{1.2} \cdot \sin\left(\frac{i}{40} \cdot \pi\right)$$

$$K_{i,j} := 8 \cdot \cos\left(\frac{j}{80} \cdot \pi\right)$$

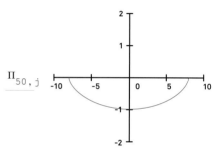

$\Pi_{50,j}$

$K_{50,j}$

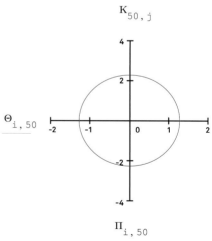

$\Theta_{i,50}$

$\Pi_{i,50}$

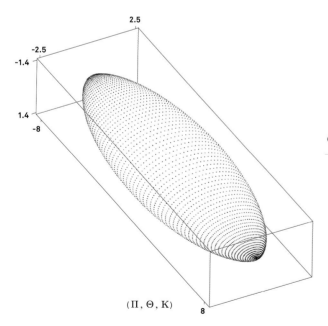

$(\Pi, \Theta, K)$

Length: 9 mm | Width: 3 mm
Cooking Time: 11 min

# QUADREFIORE

An uncommon variety of *pasta corta* (short pasta), *quadrefiori* (square flowers) are sturdy, with rippled edges running down their lengths. Francis Ford Coppola, the maker and distributor, uses antique bronze moulds and wooden drying racks to achieve an authentic form and consistency.

> STRAIGHT LONGITUDINAL PROFILE
> ⌄ HOLLOW CROSS-SECTION
> ⌄ STRIATED SURFACE
> ⌄ CRENELLATED EDGES

_ranges

$i := 0, 1 .. 500$

$j := 0, 1 .. 50$

_equations

$$\Pi_{i,j} := 2 \cdot \cos\left(\frac{i}{250} \cdot \pi\right) \cdot \left(\sin\left(\frac{3 \cdot i}{250} \cdot \pi\right)\right)^{20} + \left(0.6 + 0.9 \cdot \sin\left(\frac{j}{50} \cdot \pi\right)\right) \cdot \cos\left(\frac{i}{250} \cdot \pi\right) + 0.2 \cdot \cos\left(\frac{4 \cdot j}{25} \cdot \pi\right)$$

$$\Theta_{i,j} := 2 \cdot \sin\left(\frac{i}{250} \cdot \pi\right) \cdot \left(\sin\left(\frac{3 \cdot i}{250} \cdot \pi\right)\right)^{20} + \left(0.6 + 0.9 \cdot \sin\left(\frac{j}{50} \cdot \pi\right)\right) \cdot \sin\left(\frac{i}{250} \cdot \pi\right) + 1.5 \cdot \sin\left(\frac{j}{50} \cdot \pi\right)$$

$$K_{i,j} := \frac{3 \cdot j}{10}$$

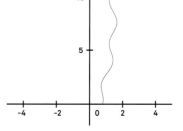

$K_{25,j}$

$\Pi_{25,j}$

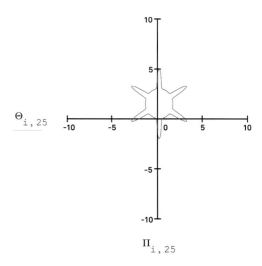

$\Theta_{i,25}$

$\Pi_{i,25}$

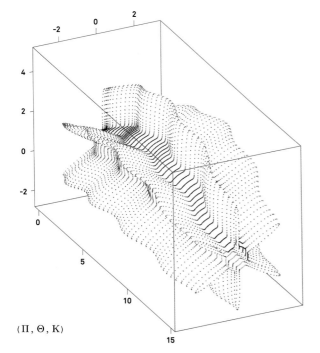

$(\Pi, \Theta, K)$

Diameter: **15 mm** | Thickness: **35 mm**
Cooking Time: **15 min**

# QUADRETTI

These flat shapes are made with durum-wheat flour, eggs and even nutmeg. *Quadretti* (tiny squares) are a classic *pastine* prepared using the leftovers of larger pasta sheets, and can be served as part of a traditional fish broth, or in soups containing fava beans. Their small shape means that they need only be cooked for a short time.

› STRAIGHT LONGITUDINAL PROFILE

⌄ SOLID CROSS-SECTION

⌄ SMOOTH SURFACE

⌄ SMOOTH EDGES

_ranges

$i := 0, 1 .. \ 70$

$j := 0, 1 .. \ 70$

_equations

$$\Pi_{i,j} := \frac{3 \cdot i}{14}$$

$$\Theta_{i,j} := \frac{3 \cdot j}{14}$$

$$K_{i,j} := 0$$

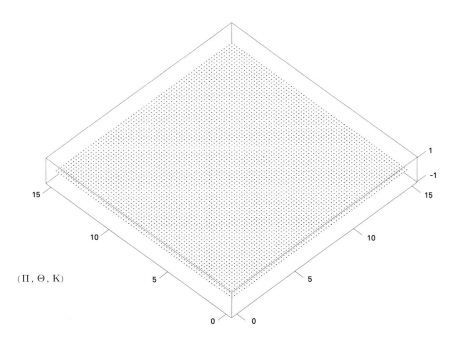

$(\Pi, \Theta, K)$

Length: **6 mm** | Width: **6 mm**
Cooking Time: **6 min**

# RACCHETTE

Usually served in salads, *racchette* (rackets) suit crunchy pine nuts, sliced asparagus and fresh peas. Alternatively, the addition of diced watermelon or pomegranate seeds can create a light-tasting snack.

> STRAIGHT LONGITUDINAL PROFILE
> ∨ HOLLOW CROSS-SECTION
> ∨ SMOOTH SURFACE
> ∨ SMOOTH EDGES

_ranges

$i := 0, 1 .. \ 3000$

$j := 0, 1 .. \ 4$

_equations

$$\alpha_i := \sin\left(\frac{i}{2000}\cdot\pi\right)^{0.5}$$

$$\Pi_{i,j} := 2\cdot\cos\left(\frac{i+1500}{1500}\cdot\pi\right) + 0.65\cdot\cos\left(\frac{i+750}{1500}\cdot\pi\right) + 2\cdot\left(\left|\cos\left(\frac{i}{300}\cdot\pi\right)\right|\right)^{100}\cos\left(\frac{i}{1500}\cdot\pi\right)$$

$$\Theta_{i,j} := 2.4\cdot\sin\left(\frac{i+1500}{1500}\cdot\pi\right) + 0.1\cdot\sin\left(\frac{i}{1500}\cdot\pi\right) + 2.3\cdot\left(\left|\sin\left(\frac{i}{300}\cdot\pi\right)\right|\right)^{100}\cdot\sin\left(\frac{i}{1500}\cdot\pi\right)$$

$$T_{i,j} := \text{if}\left[i \le 2000, 2.1\cdot\cos\left[\left(2\alpha_i+1\right)\pi\right] + 0.65\cdot\cos\left[\left(2\alpha_i+0.5\right)\pi\right] + 2.5\sin\left[\left(\alpha_i+1.83\right)\cdot\pi\right]^{500}, -2.1\right]$$

$$X_{i,j} := \text{if}\left[i \le 2000, 2.5\cdot\sin\left[\left(2\alpha_i+1\right)\pi\right] + 0.1\cdot\sin\left(\alpha_i\cdot2\pi\right) + 3\sin\left[\left(\alpha_i+1.83\right)\cdot\pi\right]^{500}, 0\right]$$

$$K_{i,j} := \frac{j}{4}$$

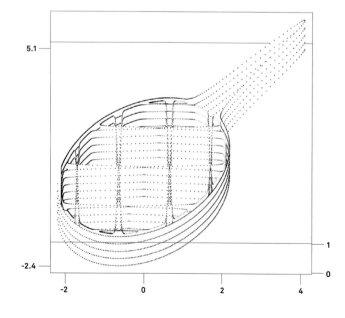

$(\Pi, \Theta, K), (T, X, K)$

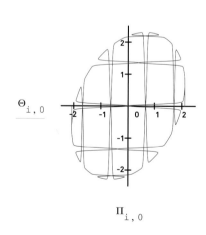

$\dfrac{\Theta_{i,0}}{\Pi_{i,0}}$

Length: 31 mm | Width: 15 mm
Cooking Time: 11 min

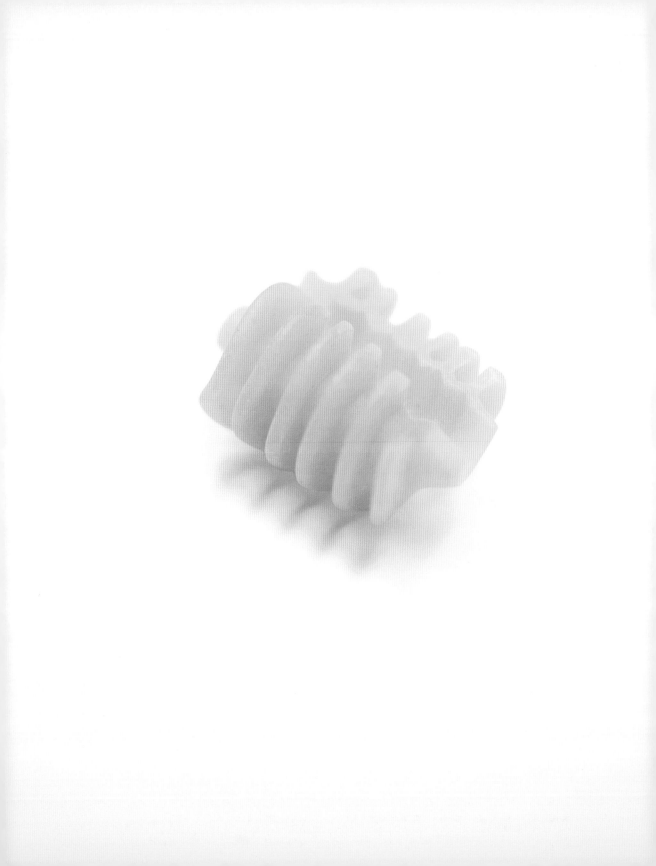

# RADIATORI

Small and squat, *radiatori* (radiators) are named after their ruffled edge. When boiled, drained and served as a *pastasciutta* their open centre and large surface area holds thick sauces well, while the flaps sweep up and trap smaller morsels of food. This pasta is often accompanied by a lamb-, veal-, rabbit- or pork-based *ragù*.

_ranges

$i := 0, 1 .. 70$

$j := 0, 1 .. 1000$

_equations

$$\Pi_{i,j} := \left[1.5 + 3 \cdot \left(\frac{i}{70}\right)^5 + 4 \cdot \sin\left(\frac{j}{200} \cdot \pi\right)^{50}\right] \cdot \cos\left(\frac{4 \cdot i}{175} \cdot \pi\right)$$

$$\Theta_{i,j} := \left[1.5 + 3 \cdot \left(\frac{i}{70}\right)^5 + 4 \cdot \sin\left(\frac{j}{200} \cdot \pi\right)^{50}\right] \cdot \sin\left(\frac{4 \cdot i}{175} \cdot \pi\right)$$

$$K_{i,j} := \frac{j}{50} + \cos\left(\frac{3 \cdot i}{14} \cdot \pi\right) \cdot \sin\left(\frac{j}{1000} \cdot \pi\right)$$

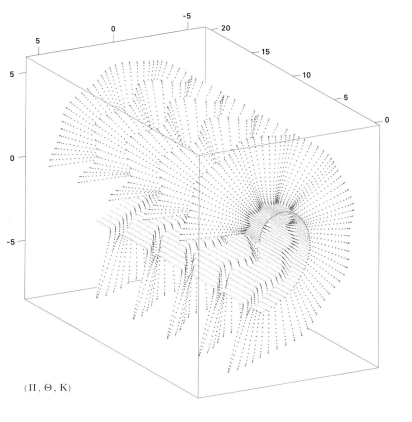

$(\Pi, \Theta, K)$

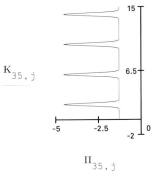

$K_{35,j}$

$\Pi_{35,j}$

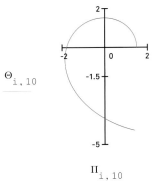

$\Theta_{i,10}$

$\Pi_{i,10}$

Length: 24 mm | Width: 17 mm
Cooking Time: 9 min

# RAVIOLI QUADRATI

Except for the square outline, *ravioli quadrati* (square *ravioli*) are made in an identical fashion to *ravioli tondi* (round *ravioli*). Other variations on the theme include crescents, triangles and hearts. Some suggest the name *ravioli* derives from the verb meaning 'to wrap', others link it with *rapa*, the Italian word for turnip.

> PINCHED LONGITUDINAL PROFILE
⌄ HOLLOW CROSS-SECTION
⌄ SMOOTH SURFACE
⌄ CRENELLATED EDGES

_ranges

$i := 0, 1 .. 100$

$j := 0, 1 .. 100$

_equations

$$\Pi_{i,j} := \frac{i}{2} + 0.4 \cdot \sin\left(\frac{j+2.5}{5} \cdot \pi\right) \cdot \left(\sin\left(\frac{i}{200} \cdot \pi\right)^{0.2} - \cos\left(\frac{i}{200} \cdot \pi\right)^{0.2}\right)$$

$$\Theta_{i,j} := \frac{j}{2} + 0.4 \cdot \sin\left(\frac{11 \cdot i + 25}{50} \cdot \pi\right) \cdot \left(\sin\left(\frac{j}{200} \cdot \pi\right)^{0.2} - \cos\left(\frac{j}{200} \cdot \pi\right)^{0.2}\right)$$

$$K_{i,j} := \text{if}\left(10 < j < 90 \wedge 10 < i < 90, \; 10 \cdot \sin\left(\frac{i-10}{80} \cdot \pi\right)^{0.6} \cdot \sin\left(\frac{j-10}{80} \cdot \pi\right)^{0.6}, \; \text{if}\,(10 > j \vee 10 > i, 0, 0)\right)$$

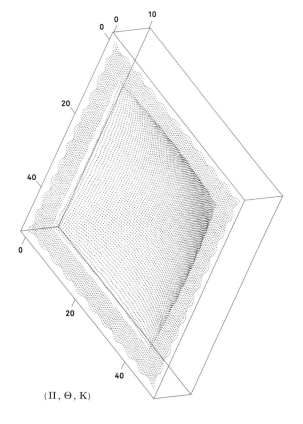

$(\Pi, \Theta, K)$

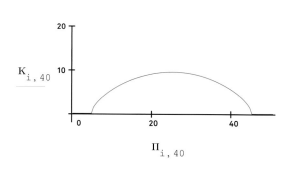

$K_{i,40}$

$\Pi_{i,40}$

Length: **50 mm** | Width: **50 mm**
Cooking Time: **5 min**

# RAVIOLI TONDI

By far the best-known *pasta ripiena* (filled pasta), *ravioli tondi* (round *ravioli*) are made by sealing a filling between two layers of dough made from wheat flour and egg. Fillings vary enormously, from lavish pairings of meat and cheese, to more delicate centres of mushrooms, spinach or even nettle.

> PINCHED LONGITUDINAL PROFILE
>> ⌄ HOLLOW CROSS-SECTION
>>> ⌄ SMOOTH SURFACE
>>>> ⌄ CRENELLATED EDGES

_ranges

$i := 0, 1 .. 80$

$j := 0, 1 .. 80$

_equations

$$\Pi_{i,j} := \frac{5 \cdot i}{8} + 0.5 \cdot \sin\left(\frac{j+2}{4} \cdot \pi\right) \cdot \left(\sin\left(\frac{i}{160} \cdot \pi\right)^{0.2} - \cos\left(\frac{i}{160} \cdot \pi\right)^{0.2}\right)$$

$$\Theta_{i,j} := \frac{5 \cdot j}{8} + 0.5 \cdot \sin\left(\frac{i+2}{4} \cdot \pi\right) \cdot \left(\sin\left(\frac{j}{160} \cdot \pi\right)^{0.2} - \cos\left(\frac{j}{160} \cdot \pi\right)^{0.2}\right)$$

$$K_{i,j} := \text{if}\left[600 \geq (i-40)^2 + (j-40)^2, 0.5 \cdot \sqrt{600 - (i-40)^2 - (j-40)^2}, 0\right]$$

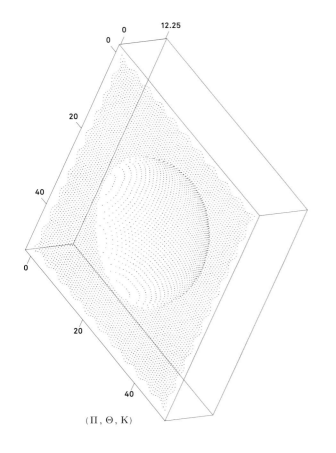

$(\Pi, \Theta, K)$

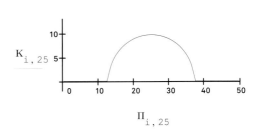

$\Pi_{i,25}$

Length: 50 mm | Width: 50 mm
Cooking Time: 5 min

# RICCIOLI

A well-known *pasta corta* (short pasta), *riccioli* (curls) originated in the Emilia-Romagna region of northern Italy. Their ribbed exterior and hollow shape mean *riccioli* can retain a large quantity of sauce.

_ranges

$i := 0, 1 .. \ 50$

$j := 0, 1 .. \ 200$

_equations

$$\Pi_{i,j} := \left( 2 + 8 \cdot \sin\left( \frac{i}{100} \cdot \pi \right) + 9 \cdot \sin\left( \frac{11 \cdot j + 100}{400} \cdot \pi \right)^2 \right) \cdot \cos\left( \frac{4 \cdot i}{125} \cdot \pi \right)$$

$$\Theta_{i,j} := \left( 2 + 8 \cdot \sin\left( \frac{i}{100} \cdot \pi \right) + 9 \cdot \sin\left( \frac{11 \cdot j + 100}{400} \cdot \pi \right)^2 \right) \cdot \sin\left( \frac{4 \cdot i}{125} \cdot \pi \right)$$

$$K_{i,j} := \frac{j}{4}$$

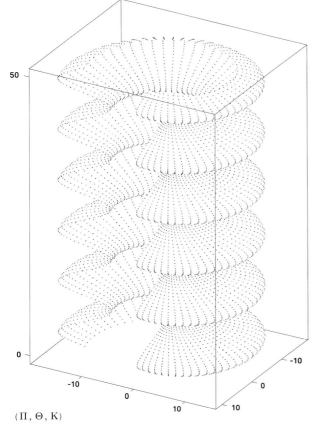

$(\Pi, \Theta, K)$

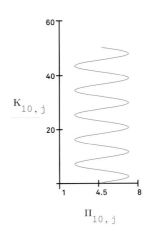

$K_{10,j}$

$\Pi_{10,j}$

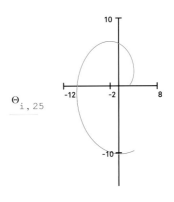

$\Theta_{i,25}$

$\Pi_{i,25}$

Length: 35 mm | Width: 15 mm
Cooking Time: 11 min

# RICCIOLI AI CINQUE SAPORI

*Riccioli* and *riccioli ai cinque sapori* (curls in five flavours) are both members of the *pasta corta* (short pasta) family, without being related by structural similarities. Made of durum-wheat flour, *riccioli ai cinque sapori* get their colour from the addition of spinach, tomato, beetroot and turmeric, and are usually served in broth.

> BENT LONGITUDINAL PROFILE
> ∨ SEMI-OPEN CROSS-SECTION
> ∨ SMOOTH SURFACE
> ∨ SMOOTH EDGES

_ranges

$i := 0, 1 .. 20$

$j := 0, 1 .. 100$

_equations

$$\Pi_{i,j} := 1.5 \cdot \cos\left(\frac{i}{20} \cdot \pi\right) \cdot \left(1 + 0.5 \cdot \sin\left(\frac{j}{25} \cdot \pi\right) \cdot \sin\left(\frac{i}{40} \cdot \pi\right) + 0.43 \cdot \sin\left(\frac{j + 18.75}{25} \cdot \pi\right) \cdot \cos\left(\frac{i}{40} \cdot \pi\right)\right) + 2 \cdot \cos\left(\frac{j}{50} \cdot \pi\right)$$

$$\Theta_{i,j} := 1.5 \cdot \sin\left(\frac{i}{20} \cdot \pi\right)^3 + \cos\left(\frac{j}{25} \cdot \pi\right)$$

$$K_{i,j} := \sin\left(\frac{j}{100} \cdot \pi\right) + 20 \cdot \cos\left(\frac{j}{200} \cdot \pi\right)^2$$

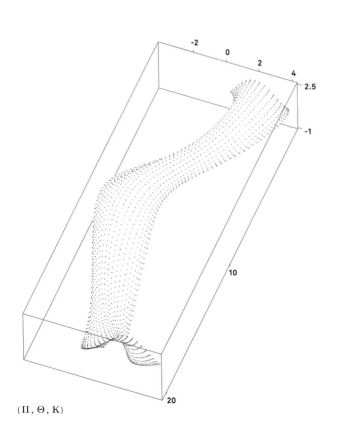

$(\Pi, \Theta, K)$

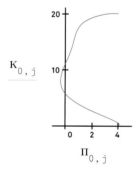

$\dfrac{K_{0,j}}{\Pi_{0,j}}$

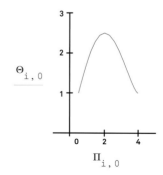

$\dfrac{\Theta_{i,0}}{\Pi_{i,0}}$

Length: 36 mm | Width: 8 mm
Cooking Time: 4–5 min

# RIGATONI

Members of the *pasta corta* (short pasta) branch, and originally from southern Italy, *rigatoni* (large ridges) are very versatile. Their robust shape holds cream or tomato sauces well, but *rigatoni* are best eaten with sausages or game meat, mushrooms and black pepper.

> STRAIGHT LONGITUDINAL PROFILE
> ⌄ HOLLOW CROSS-SECTION
> ⌄ STRIATED SURFACE
> ⌄ SMOOTH EDGES

_ranges

$i := 0, 1 .. \ 240$

$j := 0, 1 .. \ 60$

_equations

$$\Pi_{i,j} := 0.2 \cdot \sin\left(\frac{7 \cdot i + 15}{30} \cdot \pi\right) + 2 \cdot \cos\left(\frac{j + 60}{120} \cdot \pi\right) + \left[7 + \left(\frac{60 - j}{60}\right) \cdot \sin\left(\frac{i}{240} \cdot \pi\right)\right] \cdot \cos\left(\frac{i}{120} \cdot \pi\right)$$

$$\Theta_{i,j} := 0.2 \cdot \sin\left(\frac{7 \cdot i}{30} \cdot \pi\right) + \left(8 + 0.1 \cdot \frac{60 - j}{60} + \frac{j}{30} \cdot \cos\left(\frac{i}{240} \cdot \pi\right)\right) \cdot \sin\left(\frac{i}{120} \cdot \pi\right)$$

$$K_{i,j} := \frac{j}{2}$$

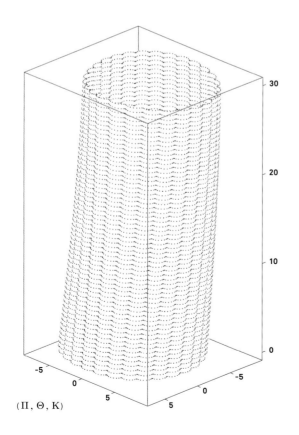

$(\Pi, \Theta, K)$

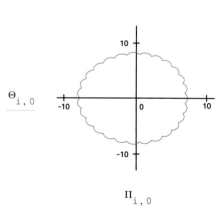

$\Theta_{i,0}$

$\Pi_{i,0}$

Length: **40 mm** | Diameter: **16 mm**
Cooking Time: **13 min**

# ROMBI

A lesser-known *pasta corta*, *rombi* (rhombuses) feature two curled edges like *lasagna doppia riccia* (page 104), however, they are smaller and sheared on the diagonal. Generally served with sauce as *pastasciutta* or *in brodo* (in broth), according to size.

> SHEARED LONGITUDINAL PROFILE

∨ SOLID CROSS-SECTION

∨ SMOOTH SURFACE

∨ CRENELLATED EDGES

_ranges

$i := 0, 1 .. 50$

$j := 0, 1 .. 50$

_equations

$$\Pi_{i,j} := \mathrm{if}\left(13 \le i \le 37, \frac{i}{20} + \frac{j}{25} - \frac{1}{20}, \mathrm{if}\left(i \le 13, \frac{3 \cdot i}{65} + \frac{j}{25}, \frac{6}{65} + \frac{3i}{65} + \frac{j}{25}\right)\right)$$

$$\Theta_{i,j} := \frac{j}{25}$$

$$K_{i,j} := \mathrm{if}\left[13 \le i \le 37, 0, \mathrm{if}\left[i \le 13, 0.2 \cdot \left(\frac{13-i}{13}\right) \cdot \cos\left(\frac{2 \cdot j + 12.5}{25} \cdot \pi\right), \frac{i-37}{65} \cdot \cos\left(\frac{2 \cdot j + 37.5}{25} \cdot \pi\right)\right]\right]$$

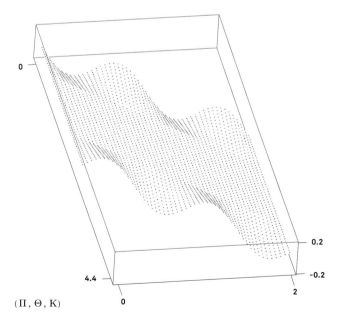

0

4.4

0

0.2

-0.2

2

$(\Pi, \Theta, K)$

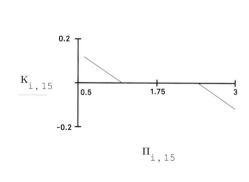

0.2

$K_{i,15}$

0.5

1.75

3

-0.2

$\Pi_{i,15}$

Length: 46 mm | Width: 24 mm
Cooking Time: 12 min

# ROTELLE

A modern design from the more unusual side of the *pasta corta* (short pasta) family, *rotelle* (small wheels) are constructed with spokes that help trap various flavours, making the pasta a good companion for a variety of sauces. Smaller versions can be served in salads or cooked in soups.

> STRAIGHT LONGITUDINAL PROFILE
> ⌄ HOLLOW CROSS-SECTION
> ⌄ STRIATED SURFACE
> ⌄ SMOOTH EDGES

_ranges

$i := 0, 1 .. 2000$

$j := 0, 1 .. 5$

_equations

$$\Pi_{i,j} := 0.5 \cdot \cos\left(\frac{i}{1000} \cdot \pi\right) + 1.5 \cdot \left(\sin\left(\frac{3 \cdot i}{1000} \cdot \pi\right)\right)^{50} \cos\left(\frac{i}{1000} \cdot \pi\right)$$

$$\Theta_{i,j} := 0.5 \cdot \sin\left(\frac{i}{1000} \cdot \pi\right) + 1.5 \cdot \left(\sin\left(\frac{3 \cdot i}{1000} \cdot \pi\right)\right)^{50} \sin\left(\frac{i}{1000} \cdot \pi\right)$$

$$T_{i,j} := \mathrm{if}\left(i \le 666, 2 \cdot \cos\left(\frac{3 \cdot i}{1000} \cdot \pi\right) + 0.03 \cdot \cos\left(\frac{93 \cdot i}{1000} \cdot \pi\right), 2.03\right)$$

$$X_{i,j} := \mathrm{if}\left(i \le 666, 2.05 \cdot \sin\left(\frac{3 \cdot i}{1000} \cdot \pi\right) + 0.03 \cdot \sin\left(\frac{93 \cdot i}{1000} \cdot \pi\right), 0\right)$$

$$K_{i,j} := \frac{j}{5}$$

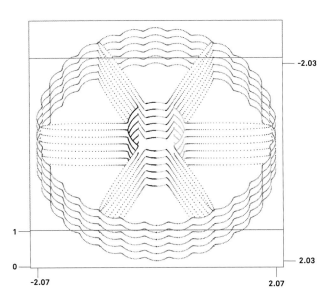

$(\Pi, \Theta, K) , (T, X, K)$

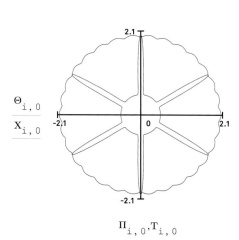

$$\frac{\Theta_{i,0}}{X_{i,0}}$$

$\Pi_{i,0}, T_{i,0}$

Diameter: 21 mm | Depth: 6 mm
Cooking Time: 12 min

# SACCOTTINI

Another out-and-out member of the *pasta ripiena* (filled pasta) club, *saccottini* – like *fagottini* (see page 060), to which they are closely related – are made of a durum-wheat circle of dough gathered into an irregular ball-shaped bundle. *Saccottini* are usually stuffed with ricotta, meat or steamed greens.

> PINCHED LONGITUDINAL PROFILE
  ˅ HOLLOW CROSS-SECTION
    ˅ SMOOTH SURFACE
      ˅ SMOOTH EDGES

_ranges

$i := 0, 1 .. \ 150$

$j := 0, 1 .. \ 100$

_equations

$$\Pi_{i,j} := \cos\left(\frac{i}{75}\cdot\pi\right)\cdot\left(\sin\left(\frac{j}{50}\cdot\pi\right) + 1.3\cdot\sin\left(\frac{j}{200}\cdot\pi\right) + \frac{3\cdot j}{1000}\cdot\cos\left(\frac{i+25}{25}\cdot\pi\right)\right)$$

$$\Theta_{i,j} := \sin\left(\frac{i}{75}\cdot\pi\right)\cdot\left[\sin\left(\frac{j}{50}\cdot\pi\right) + 1.3\cdot\sin\left(\frac{j}{200}\cdot\pi\right) + 0.7\cdot\left(\frac{j}{100}\right)^2\cdot\sin\left(\frac{i}{15}\cdot\pi\right)\right]$$

$$K_{i,j} := 2\left[1 - \left(\cos\left(\frac{j}{200}\cdot\pi\right)\right)^5 + \left(\frac{j}{100}\right)^{4.5}\right]$$

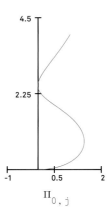

$K_{0,j}$

$\Pi_{0,j}$

$(\Pi, \Theta, K)$

Length: 30 mm | Width: 20 mm
Cooking Time: 4 min

# SAGNARELLI

This short and rectangular ribbon with four indented edges belongs to the *pasta lunga* (long pasta) branch. *Sagnarelli* are sometimes made with eggs and are generally served as *pastasciutta* with a meat *ragù*, or alongside vegetables such as wild asparagus.

> STRAIGHT LONGITUDINAL PROFILE
>> SOLID CROSS-SECTION
>>> SMOOTH SURFACE
>>>> CRENELLATED EDGES

_ranges

$i := 0, 1 .. \ 100$

$j := 0, 1 .. \ 60$

_equations

$$\alpha(x) := 0.05 \cdot \sin\left(\frac{x + 1.5}{3} \cdot \pi\right) \qquad \beta(x) := 0.05 \cdot \sin\left(\frac{9 \cdot x + 12.5}{25} \cdot \pi\right)$$

$$\Pi_{i,j} := \frac{i}{10} + \alpha(j) \cdot \left(\cos\left(\frac{i}{120} \cdot \pi\right)^{100} - \sin\left(\frac{i}{200} \cdot \pi\right)^{100}\right)$$

$$\Theta_{i,j} := \frac{j}{20} + \beta(i) \cdot \left(\cos\left(\frac{j}{120} \cdot \pi\right)^{100} - \sin\left(\frac{j}{120} \cdot \pi\right)^{100}\right)$$

$$K_{i,j} := 0$$

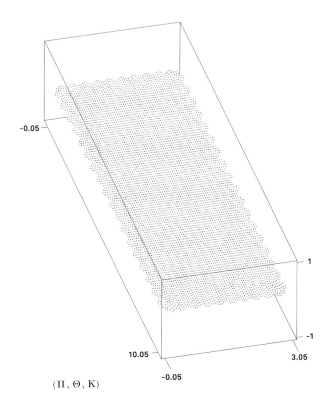

$(\Pi, \Theta, K)$

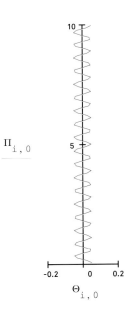

$\Pi_{i,0}$

$\Theta_{i,0}$

Length: 55 mm | Width: 20 mm
Cooking Time: 12 min

# SAGNE INCANNULATE

Shaping the twisted ribbons of durum-wheat pasta known as *sagne incannulate* requires skill. Strips of dough are held at the end against a wooden board with one hand, while the palm of the other rolls the rest of the *pasta lunga* (long pasta) to form the distinctive curl. *Sagne* are best consumed with a thick sauce or a traditional *ragù*.

> HELICOIDAL LONGITUDINAL PROFILE
∨ HOLLOW CROSS-SECTION
∨ SMOOTH SURFACE
∨ SMOOTH EDGES

_ranges

$i := 0, 1.. \ 200$

$j := 0, 1.. \ 20$

_equations

$$\Pi_{i,j} := \left(1 - 0.2 \cdot \sin\left(\frac{3 \cdot j}{20} \cdot \pi\right)\right) \cdot \cos\left(\frac{i+10}{20} \cdot \pi\right) + 2 \cdot \sin\left(\frac{i-100}{200} \cdot \pi\right) + \frac{3 \cdot i}{200} \cdot \sin\left(\frac{i}{400} \cdot \pi\right)^{200}$$

$$\Theta_{i,j} := \left(1 - 0.2 \cdot \sin\left(\frac{3 \cdot j}{20} \cdot \pi\right)\right) \cdot \sin\left(\frac{i+10}{20} \cdot \pi\right) + \sin\left(\frac{i-50}{200} \cdot \pi\right)$$

$$A_{i,j} := -3 + \left(1 - 0.1 \cdot \sin\left(\frac{3 \cdot j}{20} \cdot \pi\right)\right) \cdot \sin\left(\frac{3 \cdot i - 10}{50} \cdot \pi\right) + \cos\left(\frac{i}{200}\pi\right) + \frac{3 \cdot i}{200} \cdot \sin\left(\frac{i}{400} \cdot \pi\right)^{5}$$

$$B_{i,j} := -5 + \left(1 - 0.1 \cdot \sin\left(\frac{3 \cdot j}{20} \cdot \pi\right)\right) \cdot \cos\left(\frac{3 \cdot i + 10}{50} \cdot \pi\right) + 2 \cdot \sin\left(\frac{i}{200} \cdot \pi\right) \qquad K_{i,j} := \frac{i}{4} + \frac{7}{2} \cdot \left(1 + \cos\left(\frac{j}{20} \cdot \pi\right)\right)$$

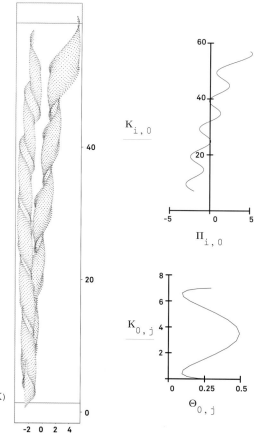

$(\Pi, \Theta, K), (A, B, K)$

Length: 250 mm | Diameter: 27 mm
Cooking Time: 14 min

# SCIALATIELLI

Hailing from the Amalfi coast in the province of Naples, *scialatielli* are a rustic *pasta lunga* (long pasta) similar in appearance to *fettuccine* and *tagliatelle* (pages 070 and 174). When they are made, milk and eggs can be added to the durum-wheat flour to lend it a golden colour. *Scialatielli* are best paired with seafood, or a *ragù* of pork or veal.

> STRAIGHT LONGITUDINAL PROFILE

⌄ SOLID CROSS-SECTION

⌄ SMOOTH SURFACE

⌄ SMOOTH EDGES

_ranges

$i := 0, 1 .. 150$

$j := 0, 1 .. 50$

_equations

$$\Pi_{i,j} := 0.1 \cdot \cos\left(\frac{i}{75} \cdot \pi\right) + 0.1 \cdot \cos\left(\frac{i+7.5}{75} \cdot \pi\right)^3 + 0.1 \cdot \sin\left(\frac{j}{50} \cdot \pi\right)$$

$$\Theta_{i,j} := 0.1 \cdot \cos\left(\frac{i}{75} \cdot \pi\right) + 0.2 \cdot \sin\left(\frac{i}{75} \cdot \pi\right)^3 + 0.1 \cdot \sin\left(\frac{j}{50} \cdot \pi\right)$$

$$K_{i,j} := \frac{3 \cdot j}{50}$$

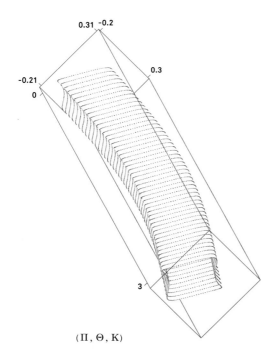

$(\Pi, \Theta, K)$

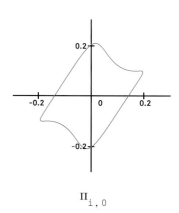

$\dfrac{\Theta_{i,0}}{\Pi_{i,0}}$

Length: 100 mm | Width: 10 mm
Cooking Time: 6 min

# SPACCATELLE

This noted speciality of Sicily belongs to the *pasta corta* (short pasta) family. *Spaccatelle* are generally elongated curves with a concave centre, and are served as a *pastasciutta* (pasta boiled and drained) with a light tomato sauce or a thick meaty *ragù*.

> BENT LONGITUDINAL PROFILE
> ∨ SEMI-OPEN CROSS-SECTION
> ∨ SMOOTH SURFACE
> ∨ SMOOTH EDGES

**_ranges**

$i := 0, 1 .. \ 25$

$j := 0, 1 .. \ 100$

**_equations**

$$\Pi_{i,j} := \left[ 0.5 + 5 \cdot \left( \frac{j}{100} \right)^3 + 0.5 \cdot \cos \left( \frac{i + 37.5}{25} \cdot \pi \right) \right] \cdot \cos \left( \frac{2 \cdot j}{125} \cdot \pi \right)$$

$$\Theta_{i,j} := 0.6 \cdot \sin \left( \frac{i + 37.5}{25} \cdot \pi \right)$$

$$K_{i,j} := \left[ 0.5 + 5 \cdot \left( \frac{j}{100} \right)^3 + 0.5 \cdot \cos \left( \frac{i + 37.5}{25} \cdot \pi \right) \right] \cdot \sin \left( \frac{2 \cdot j}{125} \cdot \pi \right)$$

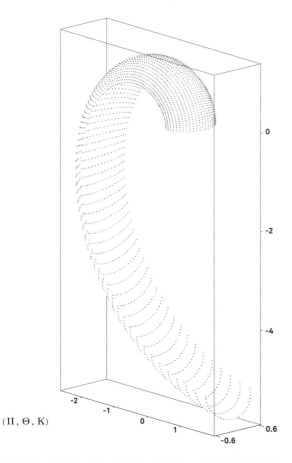

$(\Pi, \Theta, K)$

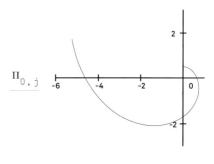

$\Pi_{0,j}$

$K_{0,j}$

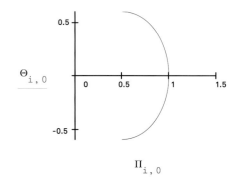

$\Theta_{i,0}$

$\Pi_{i,0}$

Length: 33 mm | Width: 7 mm
Cooking Time: 9 min

# SPAGHETTI

Without a doubt, *spaghetti* (small strings) remain the best-known and most versatile *pasta lunga* (long pasta) worldwide. Above all they are known for accompanying *ragù bolognese*, a mixture containing beef, tomato, cream, onions and pancetta. More recently, *spaghetti* have become popular in a creamy *carbonara*.

> STRAIGHT LONGITUDINAL PROFILE

∨ SOLID CROSS-SECTION

∨ SMOOTH SURFACE

∨ SMOOTH EDGES

_ranges

$i := 0, 1 .. \ 40$

$j := 0, 1 .. \ 100$

_equations

$$\Pi_{i,j} := 0.1 \cdot \cos\left(\frac{i}{20} \cdot \pi\right)$$

$$\Theta_{i,j} := 0.1 \cdot \sin\left(\frac{i}{20} \cdot \pi\right)$$

$$K_{i,j} := \frac{j}{10}$$

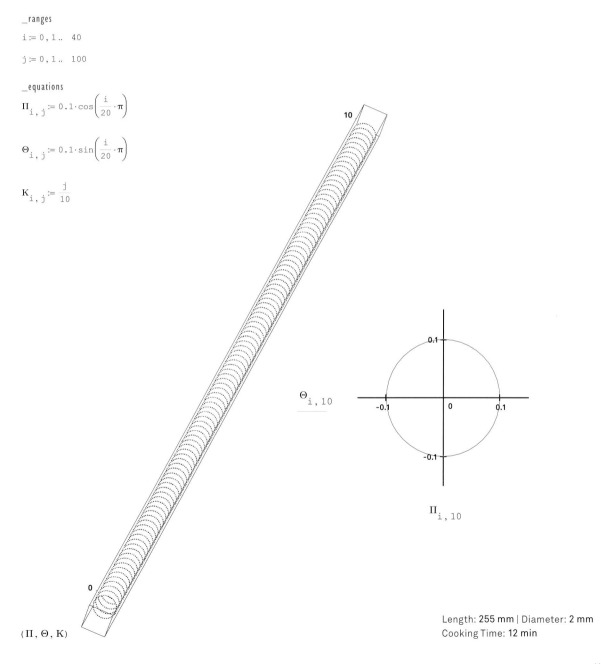

$(\Pi, \Theta, K)$

$\Theta_{i,10}$

$\Pi_{i,10}$

Length: **255 mm** | Diameter: **2 mm**
Cooking Time: **12 min**

# SPIRALI

The ridged and helicoidal *spirali* (spirals) are similar in shape to *cavatappi* (see page 039), but are slightly larger. *Spirali* may be served with chunky sauces as *pastasciutta*, baked *al forno* (at the oven) with a thick cheese topping or added to salads.

> HELICOIDAL LONGITUDINAL PROFILE
  ⌄ HOLLOW CROSS-SECTION
    ⌄ STRIATED SURFACE
      ⌄ SMOOTH EDGES

_ranges

$i := 0, 1 .. \ 100$

$j := 0, 1 .. \ 120$

_equations

$$\Pi_{i,j} := \left(2.5 + 2 \cdot \cos\left(\frac{i}{50} \cdot \pi\right) + 0.1 \cdot \cos\left(\frac{i}{5} \cdot \pi\right)\right) \cdot \cos\left(\frac{j}{30} \cdot \pi\right)$$

$$\Theta_{i,j} := \left(2.5 + 2 \cdot \cos\left(\frac{i}{50} \cdot \pi\right) + 0.1 \cdot \cos\left(\frac{i}{5} \cdot \pi\right)\right) \cdot \sin\left(\frac{j}{30} \cdot \pi\right)$$

$$\mathrm{K}_{i,j} := \left(2.5 + 2 \cdot \sin\left(\frac{i}{50} \cdot \pi\right) + 0.1 \cdot \sin\left(\frac{i}{5} \cdot \pi\right)\right) + \frac{j}{6}$$

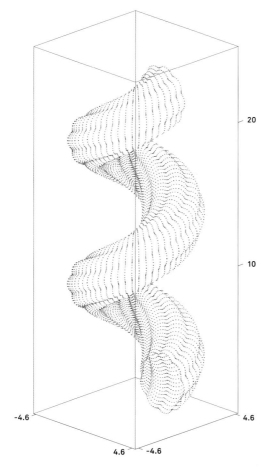

$(\Pi, \Theta, \mathrm{K})$

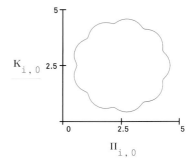

$\mathrm{K}_{i,0}$ / $\Pi_{i,0}$

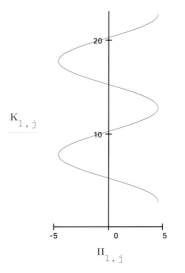

$\mathrm{K}_{1,j}$ / $\Pi_{1,j}$

Length: 33 mm | Width: 15 mm
Cooking Time: 7–9 min

# STELLETTE

A member of the *pastine minute* (tiny pasta) family, *stellette* (little stars) are only marginally larger than both *acini di pepe* and *cuoretti* (see pages 015 and 057). Like all *pastine,* they are best served in a light soup, perhaps flavoured with portobello mushrooms or peas.

> STRAIGHT LONGITUDINAL PROFILE
ᵛ HOLLOW CROSS-SECTION
ᵛ SMOOTH SURFACE
ᵛ SMOOTH EDGES

_ranges

$i := 0, 1 .. 25$

$j := 0, 1 .. 150$

_equations

$$\Pi_{i,j} := \left(3 + \frac{3 \cdot i}{5}\right) \cdot \cos\left(\frac{j}{75} \cdot \pi\right) + \frac{i}{10} \cdot \cos\left(\frac{j+15}{15} \cdot \pi\right)$$

$$\Theta_{i,j} := \left(3 + \frac{3 \cdot i}{5}\right) \cdot \sin\left(\frac{j}{75} \cdot \pi\right) + \frac{i}{10} \cdot \sin\left(\frac{j}{15} \cdot \pi\right)$$

$$K_{i,j} := 0$$

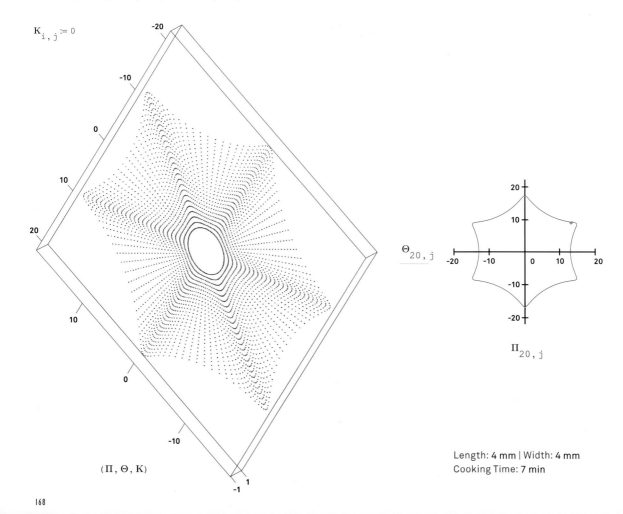

$(\Pi, \Theta, K)$

$\Theta_{20, j}$

$\Pi_{20, j}$

Length: 4 mm | Width: 4 mm
Cooking Time: 7 min

# STORTINI

Another *pastine minute* (tiny pasta), *stortini* (little crooked pieces) are consumed in creamy soups with mushroom and celery. As a rule of thumb, smaller pasta is best in thinner soups, while larger *pastina minute* can be served with thicker varieties.

> STRAIGHT LONGITUDINAL PROFILE
>> ∨ SOLID CROSS-SECTION
>>> ∨ SMOOTH SURFACE
>>>> ∨ SMOOTH EDGES

_ranges

$i := 0, 1 .. 500$

$j := 0, 1 .. 10$

_equations

$$\alpha_{i,j} := 0.5 \cdot \left( \left| \sin\left( \frac{2 \cdot i}{125} \cdot \pi \right) \right| \right)^3 \qquad \beta_{i,j} := 1 - \left| \sin\left( \frac{2 \cdot i - 500}{125} \cdot \pi \right) \right|$$

$$\gamma_{i,j} := 1 - 0.5 \cdot \left[ \left| \sin\left[ \frac{2 \cdot (i - 375)}{125} \cdot \pi \right] \right| \right]^3$$

$$\Pi_{i,j} := \text{if}\left( i \le 250, \cos\left( \frac{2 \cdot i}{125} \cdot \pi \right), 1.7 - \cos\left( \frac{2 \cdot i - 500}{125} \cdot \pi \right) \right)$$

$$\Theta_{i,j} := \text{if}\left[ i \le 250, \text{if}\left[ i \le 125, \left( \left| \sin\left( \frac{2 \cdot i}{125} \cdot \pi \right) \right| \right), \alpha_{i,j} \right], \text{if}\left( i \le 375, \beta_{i,j}, \gamma_{i,j} \right) \right]$$

$$K_{i,j} := \frac{j}{20}$$

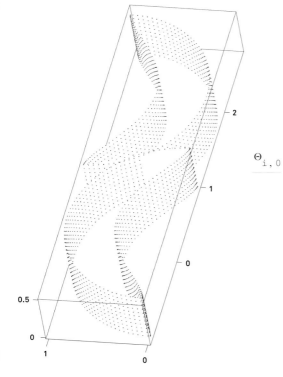

$(\Pi, \Theta, K)$

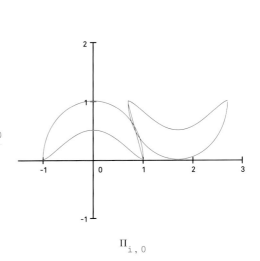

$\Theta_{i,0}$

$\Pi_{i,0}$

Length: 10 mm | Width: 3 mm
Cooking Time: 8 min

# STROZZAPRETI

The dough used to make *strozzapreti* (or *strangolapreti*: both translate as 'priest stranglers') can be prepared with assorted flours, eggs and even potato. *Strozzapreti* are an ideal *pastasciutta*, and can be served with a traditional meat sauce, topped with Parmigiano-Reggiano.

> TWISTED LONGITUDINAL PROFILE
> ⌄ SEMI-OPEN CROSS-SECTION
> ⌄ SMOOTH SURFACE
> ⌄ SMOOTH EDGES

_ranges

$i := 0, 1 .. \ 60$

$j := 0, 1 .. \ 60$

_equations

$$\alpha_{i,j} := 0.5 \cdot \cos\left(\frac{j}{40} \cdot \pi\right) + 0.5 \cdot \cos\left(\frac{j+76}{40} \cdot \pi\right) + 0.5 \cdot \cos\left(\frac{j}{30} \cdot \pi\right) + 0.5 \cdot \sin\left(\frac{2 \cdot i - j}{40} \cdot \pi\right)$$

$$\beta_{i,j} := 0.5 \cdot \sin\left(\frac{j}{40} \cdot \pi\right) + 0.5 \cdot \sin\left(\frac{j+76}{40} \cdot \pi\right) + 0.5 \cdot \sin\left(\frac{j}{30} \cdot \pi\right) + 0.5 \cdot \cos\left(\frac{2 \cdot i - j}{40} \cdot \pi\right)$$

$$\Pi_{i,j} := \text{if}\left(i \leq 30, 0.5 \cdot \cos\left(\frac{j}{30} \cdot \pi\right) + 0.5 \cdot \cos\left(\frac{2 \cdot i + j + 16}{40} \cdot \pi\right), \alpha_{i,j}\right)$$

$$\Theta_{i,j} := \text{if}\left(i \leq 30, 0.5 \cdot \sin\left(\frac{j}{30} \cdot \pi\right) + 0.5 \cdot \sin\left(\frac{2 \cdot i + j + 16}{40} \cdot \pi\right), \beta_{i,j}\right)$$

$$K_{i,j} := \frac{j}{4}$$

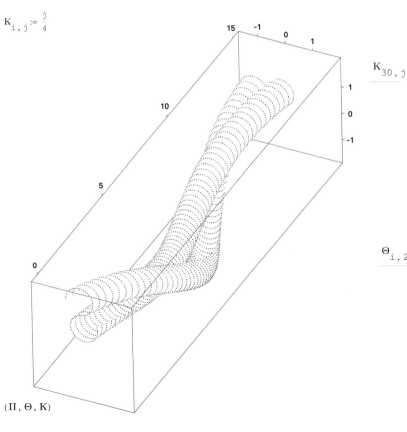

$(\Pi, \Theta, K)$

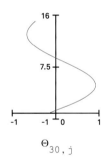

$\dfrac{K_{30,j}}{\Theta_{30,j}}$

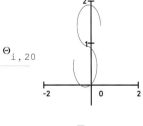

$\dfrac{\Theta_{i,20}}{\Pi_{i,20}}$

Length: 53 mm | Width: 7 mm
Cooking Time: 11 min

# TAGLIATELLE

A mixture of wheat-flour and eggs, *tagliatelle* (deriving from the Italian *tagliare* – 'to cut') belong to the *pasta lunga* (long pasta) family. Originally hailing from the north of Italy, *tagliatelle* are frequently served in *carbonara* sauce, but can also accompany seafood, or alternatively may form the basis of a *timballo* (baked pasta dish).

> BENT LONGITUDINAL PROFILE
> ⌄ SOLID CROSS-SECTION
> ⌄ SMOOTH SURFACE
> ⌄ SMOOTH EDGES

_ranges

$i := 0, 1 .. \ 1000$

$j := 0, 1 .. \ 4$

_equations

$$\Pi_{i,j} := 0.4 \cdot \cos\left(\frac{3 \cdot i}{250} \cdot \pi\right) + \frac{j}{80} \cdot \sin\left(\frac{31 \cdot i}{1000} \cdot \pi\right)$$

$$T_{i,j} := 0.4 \cdot \cos\left(\frac{3 \cdot i}{250} \cdot \pi\right) + \frac{j}{80} \cdot \sin\left(\frac{31 \cdot i}{1000} \cdot \pi\right)$$

$$\Theta_{i,j} := 0.4 \cdot \sin\left(\frac{3 \cdot i}{250} \cdot \pi\right) \cdot \sin\left(\frac{i}{4000} \cdot \pi\right)^{0.1}$$

$$X_{i,j} := 0.4 \cdot \sin\left(\frac{i}{4000} \cdot \pi\right)^{0.5} \cdot \sin\left(\frac{3 \cdot i}{250} \cdot \pi\right)$$

$$K_{i,j} := \frac{j}{80} + 0.12 \cdot \sin\left(\frac{9 \cdot i}{1000} \cdot \pi\right)$$

$$\Psi_{i,j} := \frac{j}{80} + 0.12 \cdot \sin\left(\frac{9 \cdot i}{1000} \cdot \pi\right)$$

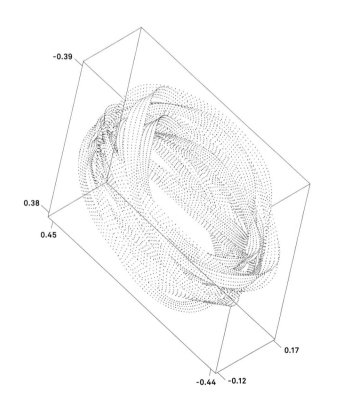

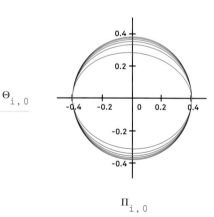

$\Theta_{i,0}$

$\Pi_{i,0}$

$(\Pi, \Theta, K) , (0.8T, 1X, 0.9\Psi) , (1T, 0.9X, 0.6\Psi)$

Width: 6 mm | Diameter: 65 mm
Cooking Time: 5 min

# TAGLIERINI

Another coiling *pasta lunga* (long pasta), *taglierini* are of the same lineage as *tagliatelle*, but are substantially narrower – almost hair-like.

› BENT LONGITUDINAL PROFILE

⌄ SOLID CROSS-SECTION

⌄ SMOOTH SURFACE

⌄ SMOOTH EDGES

_ranges

$i := 0, 1 .. 1000$

$j := 0, 1 .. 2$

_equations

$$\Pi_{i,j} := 0.5 \cdot \cos\left(\frac{i}{100} \cdot \pi\right) + 0.05 \cdot \cos\left(\frac{i}{40} \cdot \pi\right)$$

$$\Theta_{i,j} := 0.5 \cdot \sin\left(\frac{i}{4000} \cdot \pi\right)^{0.1} \cdot \sin\left(\frac{i}{100} \cdot \pi\right) + 0.075 \cdot \sin\left(\frac{i}{40} \cdot \pi\right)$$

$$K_{i,j} := \frac{3 \cdot j}{200} + 0.1 \cdot \sin\left(\frac{i}{125} \cdot \pi\right)$$

$$T_{i,j} := 0.4 \cdot \cos\left(\frac{i}{100} \cdot \pi\right) \qquad N_{i,j} := 0.3 \cdot \cos\left(\frac{i}{100} \cdot \pi\right)$$

$$X_{i,j} := 0.4 \cdot \sin\left(\frac{i}{4000} \cdot \pi\right)^{0.2} \cdot \sin\left(\frac{i}{100} \cdot \pi\right) \qquad \Xi_{i,j} := 0.3 \cdot \sin\left(\frac{3 \cdot i}{1000} \cdot \pi\right) \cdot \sin\left(\frac{i}{50} \cdot \pi\right)$$

$$\Psi_{i,j} := \frac{3 \cdot j}{200} + 0.1 \cdot \sin\left(\frac{i}{125} \cdot \pi\right) \qquad O_{i,j} := -0.05 + \frac{3 \cdot j}{200} + 0.1 \cdot \sin\left(\frac{i}{125} \cdot \pi\right)$$

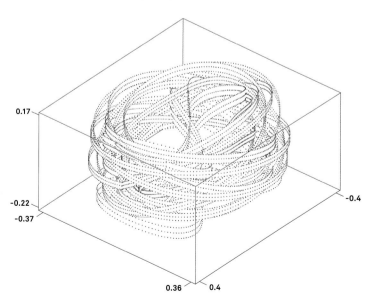

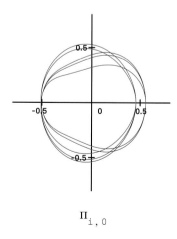

$$\frac{\Theta_{i,0}}{}$$

$$\Pi_{i,0}$$

$(\Pi \cdot 0.6, \Theta \cdot 0.5, K)$ , $(T, X, \Psi)$ , $(0.8 \cdot T, 0.9 \cdot X, 1.3\Psi)$ , $(N, 0.9\Xi, 1.5O)$

Width: 2 mm | Diameter: 70 mm
Cooking Time: 4 min

# TAGLIOLINI

Thinner even than *taglierini*, *tagliolini* are traditionally eaten as a starter with butter, soft cheese or *al pomodoro* (in a light tomato sauce). Alternatively, they may be served in a chicken broth. A versatile pasta, *tagliolini* are also the main ingredient for a variety of *timballo* dishes baked *al forno* (at the oven).

> BENT LONGITUDINAL PROFILE
> SOLID CROSS-SECTION
> SMOOTH SURFACE
> SMOOTH EDGES

_ranges

$i := 0, 1 .. \ 2000$

$j := 0, 1 .. \ 1$

_equations

$$\Pi_{i,j} := 0.5 \cdot \cos\left(\frac{i}{200} \cdot \pi\right) + 0.05 \cdot \cos\left(\frac{5 \cdot i}{400} \cdot \pi\right)$$

$$\Theta_{i,j} := 0.5 \cdot \sin\left(\frac{i}{8000} \cdot \pi\right)^{0.1} \cdot \sin\left(\frac{i}{200} \cdot \pi\right) + 0.075 \cdot \sin\left(\frac{5 \cdot i}{400} \cdot \pi\right)$$

$$K_{i,j} := 0.01 \cdot j + 0.1 \cdot \sin\left(\frac{i}{250} \cdot \pi\right)$$

$$T_{i,j} := 0.4 \cdot \cos\left(\frac{i}{200} \cdot \pi\right) \qquad N_{i,j} := 0.3 \cdot \cos\left(\frac{i}{125} \cdot \pi\right)$$

$$X_{i,j} := 0.4 \cdot \sin\left(\frac{i}{8000} \cdot \pi\right)^{0.2} \cdot \sin\left(\frac{i}{200} \cdot \pi\right) \qquad \Xi_{i,j} := 0.3 \cdot \sin\left(\frac{3 \cdot i}{2000} \cdot \pi\right) \cdot \sin\left(\frac{3 \cdot i}{200} \cdot \pi\right)$$

$$\Psi_{i,j} := 0.01 \cdot j + 0.1 \cdot \sin\left(\frac{i}{250} \cdot \pi\right) \qquad O_{i,j} := -0.05 + 0.01 \cdot j + 0.1 \cdot \sin\left(\frac{i}{250} \cdot \pi\right)$$

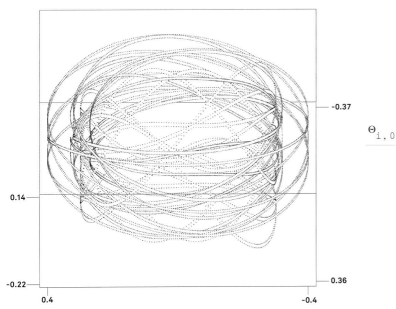

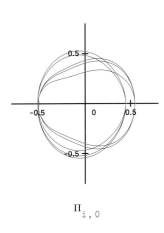

$\Theta_{i,0}$

$\Pi_{i,0}$

$(\Pi \cdot 0.6, \Theta \cdot 0.5, K), (T, X, \Psi), (0.8 \cdot T, 0.9 \cdot X, 1.3 \Psi), (N, 0.9 \Xi, 1.5 O)$

Width: 1 mm | Diameter: 60 mm
Cooking Time: 3 min

# TORCHIETTI

The whorls of *torchietti* (tiny torches) trap chunky sauces well. Also
known as *maccheroni al torchio*, they are best eaten in a tomato
sauce with larger, coarsely chopped vegetables such as carrots,
broccoli and cauliflower.

> BENT LONGITUDINAL PROFILE
∨ HOLLOW CROSS-SECTION
∨ STRIATED SURFACE
∨ SMOOTH EDGES

_ranges

$i := 0, 1 .. 40$

$j := 0, 1 .. 100$

_equations

$$\alpha_{i,j} := \frac{(3 \cdot i - 60) \cdot j}{100}$$

$$\beta_{i,j} := \frac{(3 \cdot i - 60) \cdot (100 - j)}{100}$$

$$\gamma_{i,j} := \frac{3 \cdot (i - 20) \cdot (100 - j)}{100}$$

$$\zeta_{i,j} := \frac{3 \cdot (i - 20) \cdot j}{100}$$

$$\eta_{i,j} := \mathrm{if}\left(j \le 50 \wedge i \le 20, \alpha_{i,j}, \mathrm{if}\left(j \ge 50 \wedge i \le 20, \beta_{i,j}, \mathrm{if}\left(j \ge 50 \wedge i \ge 20, \gamma_{i,j}, \zeta_{i,j}\right)\right)\right)$$

$$\iota_{i,j} := \left(3 + 2.5 \cdot \sin\left(\frac{-\eta_{i,j}}{120} \cdot \pi\right) + 3 \cdot \sin\left(\frac{j}{200} \cdot \pi\right)^{10}\right)$$

$$\Pi_{i,j} := \iota_{i,j} \cdot \cos\left(\frac{\eta_{i,j}}{10} \cdot \pi\right) + 0.1 \cdot \cos\left(\frac{j}{2} \cdot \pi\right)$$

$$\Theta_{i,j} := \iota_{i,j} \cdot \sin\left(\frac{\eta_{i,j}}{10} \cdot \pi\right) + 0.1 \cdot \sin\left(\frac{j}{2} \cdot \pi\right) + 3 \cdot \sin\left(\frac{j}{50} \cdot \pi\right)$$

$$K_{i,j} := \frac{18 \cdot j}{25} + \frac{2}{5} \cdot \eta_{i,j}$$

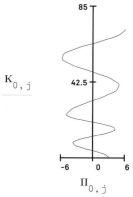

$\dfrac{K_{0,j}}{\Pi_{0,j}}$

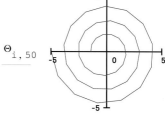

$\dfrac{\Theta_{i,50}}{\Pi_{i,50}}$

$(\Pi, \Theta, K)$

Length: 47 mm | Width: 8 mm
Cooking Time: 10–12 min

# TORTELLINI

To prepare a *tortellino*, a teaspoonful of meat, cheese or vegetables is wrapped in a layer of dough (made of wheat flour and egg) that is then skilfully rolled and folded. These shapely members of the *pasta ripiena* (filled pasta) family are traditionally eaten in steaming soups, but are also drained and served with a local sauce as *pastasciutta*.

> PINCHED LONGITUDINAL PROFILE

∨ HOLLOW CROSS-SECTION

∨ SMOOTH SURFACE

∨ SMOOTH EDGES

_ranges

$i := 0, 1 .. \ 120$

$j := 0, 1 .. \ 60$

_equations

$$\alpha_{i,j} := 0.2 \cdot \sin\left(\frac{i}{120} \cdot \pi\right) + \frac{j}{400} \qquad \beta_{i,j} := \cos\left[\frac{j}{60} \cdot \left(2.7 + 0.2 \cdot \sin\left(\frac{i}{120} \cdot \pi\right)^{50}\right) \cdot \pi + 1.4 \cdot \pi\right]$$

$$\gamma_{i,j} := \sin\left[\frac{j}{60} \cdot \left(2.7 + 0.2 \cdot \sin\left(\frac{i}{120} \cdot \pi\right)^{50}\right) \cdot \pi + 1.4 \cdot \pi\right]$$

$$\Pi_{i,j} := 0.5^{1 + 0.5 \cdot \sin\left(\frac{i}{120} \cdot \pi\right)} \cdot \cos\left(\frac{11 \cdot i - 60}{600} \cdot \pi\right) \cdot \left[1.35 + \left(3 + \sin\left(\frac{i}{120} \cdot \pi\right)\right) \cdot \alpha_{i,j} \cdot \beta_{i,j}\right]$$

$$\Theta_{i,j} := 0.5 \cdot \sin\left(\frac{11 \cdot i - 60}{600} \cdot \pi\right) \cdot \left[1.35 + \left(0.6 + \sin\left(\frac{i}{120} \cdot \pi\right)\right) \cdot \alpha_{i,j} \cdot \beta_{i,j}\right]$$

$$K_{i,j} := 0.15 + \frac{i}{1200} + 0.5 \cdot \left(0.8 \cdot \sin\left(\frac{i}{120} \cdot \pi\right) + \frac{j}{400}\right) \cdot \sin\left(\frac{i}{120} \cdot \pi\right) \cdot \gamma_{i,j}$$

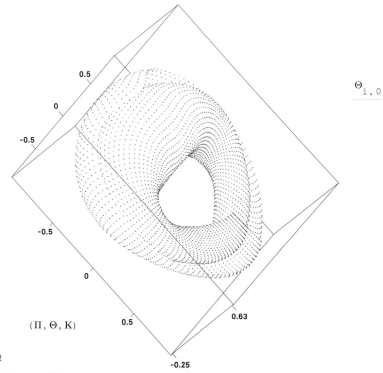

$(\Pi, \Theta, K)$

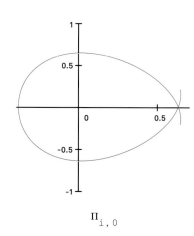

$$\frac{\Theta_{i,0}}{\Pi_{i,0}}$$

Length: 20 mm | Width: 16 mm
Cooking Time: 11–12 min

# TORTIGLIONI

Another classic *pasta corta* (short pasta), *tortiglioni* originate from the Campania region of southern Italy. *Tortiglioni* (deriving from the Italian *torquere* – 'to cut') are often baked in a *timballo*, or boiled, drained and served as a *pastasciutta* coupled with a strong sauce of tomato, chorizo and black pepper.

› STRAIGHT LONGITUDINAL PROFILE

ᵛ HOLLOW CROSS-SECTION

ᵛ STRIATED SURFACE

ᵛ SMOOTH EDGES

_ranges

$i := 0, 1.. \ 150$

$j := 0, 1.. \ 50$

_equations

$$\Pi_{i,j} := 6 \cdot \cos\left(\frac{i}{75} \cdot \pi\right) - 3.5 \cdot \cos\left(\frac{j}{100} \cdot \pi\right) + 0.15 \cdot \sin\left[\left(\frac{13 \cdot i}{75} + \frac{j}{15} + 1.5\right) \cdot \pi\right]$$

$$\Theta_{i,j} := 6 \cdot \sin\left(\frac{i}{75} \cdot \pi\right) + 0.15 \cdot \sin\left[\left(\frac{13 \cdot i}{75} + \frac{j}{15}\right) \cdot \pi\right]$$

$$K_{i,j} := \frac{11 \cdot j}{10}$$

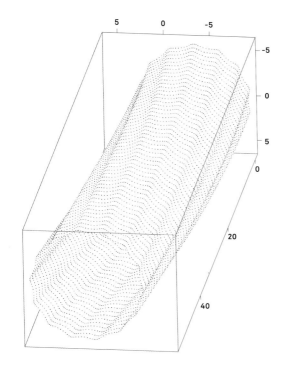

$(\Pi, \Theta, K)$

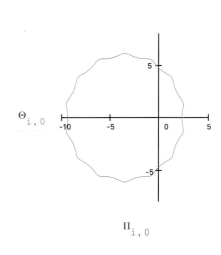

$\Theta_{i,0}$

$\Pi_{i,0}$

Length: **45 mm** | Diameter: **10 mm**
Cooking Time: **12 min**

# TRENNE

A hollow triangular variety of *pasta corta* (short pasta), *trenne* (*penne* with a triangular cross-section) are extremely sturdy. They are best served with mushrooms, tomato and spinach – or in any sauce that would normally accompany their close cousins: *penne*, *trennette* and *ziti*.

> SHEARED LONGITUDINAL PROFILE
⌄ HOLLOW CROSS-SECTION
⌄ SMOOTH SURFACE
⌄ SMOOTH EDGES

_ranges

$i := 0, 1 .. 100$

$j := 0, 1 .. 40$

_equations

$$\Pi_{i,j} := \text{if}\left(i \le 33, \frac{3 \cdot i}{10}, \frac{300 - 3 \cdot i}{20}\right)$$

$$\Theta_{i,j} := \text{if}\left(i \le 33, 0, \text{if}\left(i \le 66, \frac{9 \cdot i - 300}{20}, \frac{900 - 9 \cdot i}{20}\right)\right)$$

$$K_{i,j} := \text{if}\left(i \le 33, \text{if}\left(i \le 16, \frac{-9 \cdot i}{50} + \frac{6 \cdot j}{4}, -6 + \frac{9 \cdot i}{50} + \frac{3 \cdot j}{2}\right), \text{if}\left(i \le 66, -12 + \frac{7 \cdot i}{20} + \frac{6 \cdot j}{4}, 35 - \frac{7 \cdot i}{20} + \frac{6 \cdot j}{4}\right)\right)$$

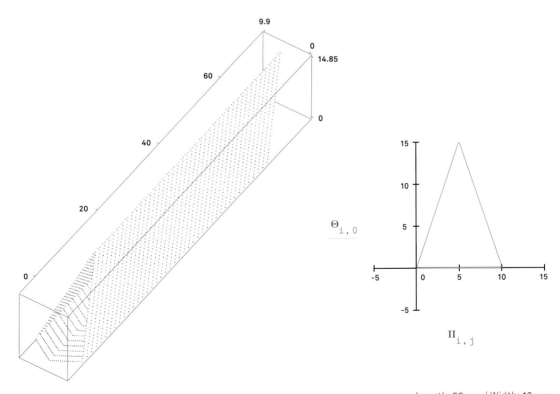

$(\Pi, \Theta, K)$

$\Theta_{i,0}$

$\Pi_{i,j}$

Length: 58 mm | Width: 13 mm
Cooking Time: 11 min

# TRIPOLINE

The ribbon-like *tripoline* are *pasta lunga* (long pasta) curled along one edge only. This wave gives the *tripoline* a varying texture after cooking, and helps them to gather extra sauce. Originally from southern Italy, they are often served with tomato and basil, or *ragù alla napoletana* and a sprinkling of Pecorino Romano.

> STRAIGHT LONGITUDINAL PROFILE
> ⌄ SOLID CROSS-SECTION
> ⌄ SMOOTH SURFACE
> ⌄ CRENELLATED EDGES

_ranges

$i := 0, 1 .. \ 40$

$j := 0, 1 .. \ 200$

_equations

$$\Pi_{i,j} := \frac{i}{20}$$

$$\Theta_{i,j} := \frac{j}{20}$$

$$K_{i,j} := if\left(i \le 30, 0, if\left(i \le 10, \frac{10-i}{50} \cdot \cos\left(\frac{j+2}{4} \cdot \pi\right), \frac{i-30}{50} \cdot \cos\left(\frac{j+15}{10} \cdot \pi\right)\right)\right)$$

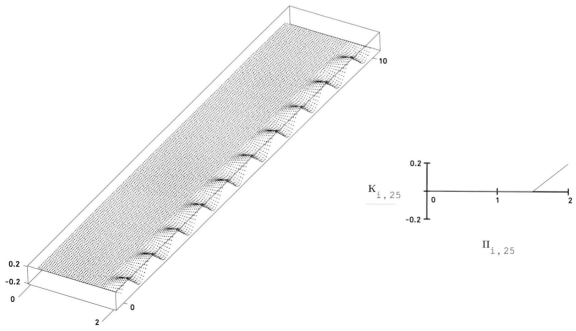

$(\Pi, \Theta, K)$

Length: 257 mm | Width: 8 mm
Cooking Time: 9 min

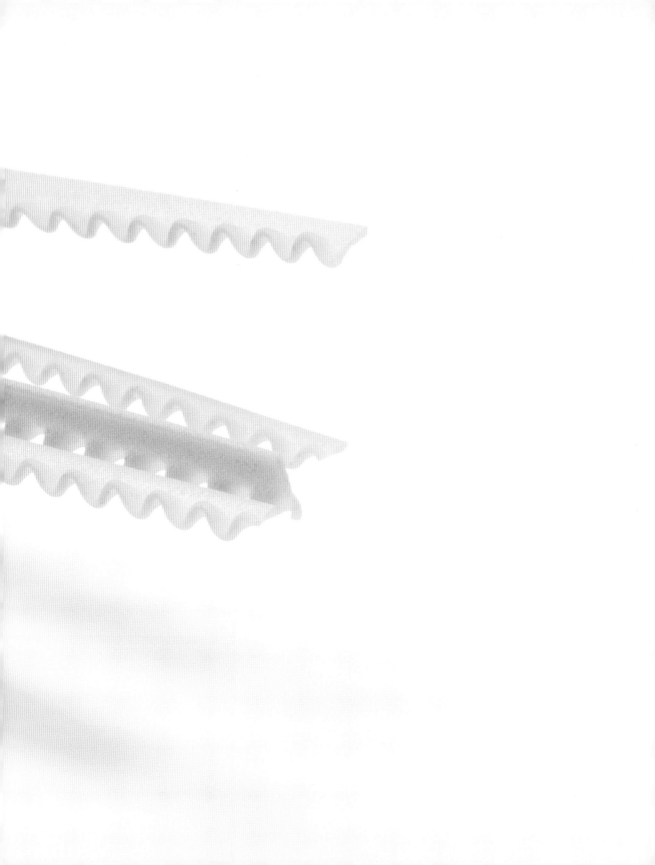

# TROFIE

The Ligurian version of *gnocchi*, *trofie* are made from a mixture of
wheat flour, bran, water and potatoes. Traditionally served boiled
with green beans and more potatoes, they may also be paired with
a simple mix of *pesto genovese*, pine nuts, salt and olive oil.

> TWISTED LONGITUDINAL PROFILE

⌄ SOLID CROSS-SECTION

⌄ SMOOTH SURFACE

⌄ SMOOTH EDGES

_ranges

$i := 0, 1 .. 150$

$j := 0, 1 .. 50$

_equations

$$\alpha_{i,j} := \frac{3 \cdot i}{5} + 10 \cdot \cos\left(\frac{j}{25} \cdot \pi\right) \qquad \Pi_{i,j} := \left(1 + \sin\left(\frac{i}{150} \cdot \pi\right) + 2 \cdot \sin\left(\frac{i}{150} \cdot \pi\right) \cdot \sin\left(\frac{j}{25} \cdot \pi\right)\right) \sin\left(\frac{13 \cdot i}{300} \cdot \pi\right)$$

$$\Theta_{i,j} := \left(1 + \sin\left(\frac{i}{150} \cdot \pi\right) + 2 \cdot \sin\left(\frac{i}{150} \cdot \pi\right) \cdot \sin\left(\frac{j}{25} \cdot \pi\right)\right) \cdot \cos\left(\frac{13 \cdot i}{300} \cdot \pi\right) + 5 \cdot \sin\left(\frac{2\alpha_{i,j}}{125} \cdot \pi\right) \qquad K_{i,j} := \alpha_{i,j}$$

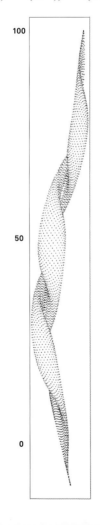

$(\Pi, \Theta, K)$

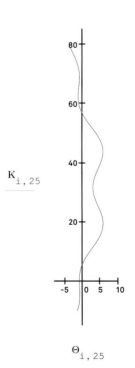

$K_{i,25}$

$\Theta_{i,25}$

Length: 50 mm | Width: 4 mm
Cooking Time: 18 min

# TROTTOLE

A well-formed *pasta corta* (short pasta) comprised of rings that curl up about a central stalk, *trottole* are ideal for salads. They are also delicious with pumpkin or courgette, leek, pine nuts and a few shavings of Parmigiano-Reggiano.

> HELICOIDAL LONGITUDINAL PROFILE
> ⌄ HOLLOW CROSS-SECTION
> ⌄ SMOOTH SURFACE
> ⌄ SMOOTH EDGES

_ranges

$i := 0, 1 .. 160$

$j := 0, 1 .. 60$

_equations

$$\alpha_{i,j} := 0.17 - 0.15 \cdot \sin\left(\frac{j}{120} \cdot \pi\right) + 0.25 \cdot \left(\frac{60-j}{60}\right)^{10} \cdot \sin\left(\frac{j}{30} \cdot \pi\right)$$

$$\gamma_{i,j} := 0.25 \cdot \left(\frac{60-j}{60}\right)^{5} \cdot \left(1 - \sin\left(\frac{i-128}{160} \cdot \pi\right)\right) \cdot \cos\left(\frac{j}{30} \cdot \pi\right)$$

$$\beta_{i,j} := 0.17 - 0.15 \cdot \sin\left(\frac{j}{120} \cdot \pi\right) + 0.25 \cdot \left(\frac{60-j}{60}\right)^{10} \cdot \sin\left(\frac{j}{30} \cdot \pi\right)$$

$$\zeta_{i,j} := \frac{7 \cdot i}{400} - \frac{48}{25} + \gamma_{i,j} + \frac{j}{120} \cdot \left(1 - \sin\left(\frac{i-128}{64} \cdot \pi\right)\right)$$

$$\Pi_{i,j} := \text{if}\left[i \geq 128, \left[\alpha_{i,j} \cdot \left(1 - \sin\left(\frac{i-128}{320} \cdot \pi\right)\right)\right] \cdot \cos\left(\frac{7 \cdot i}{160} \cdot \pi\right), \beta_{i,j} \cdot \cos\left(\frac{7 \cdot i}{160} \cdot \pi\right)\right]$$

$$\Theta_{i,j} := \text{if}\left[i \geq 128, \left[\alpha_{i,j} \cdot \left(1 - \sin\left(\frac{i-128}{160} \cdot \pi\right)\right)\right] \cdot \sin\left(\frac{7 \cdot i}{160} \cdot \pi\right), \beta_{i,j} \cdot \sin\left(\frac{7 \cdot i}{160} \cdot \pi\right)\right]$$

$$K_{i,j} := \text{if}\left[i \geq 128, \zeta_{i,j}, \frac{i}{400} + \frac{j}{100} + 0.25 \cdot \left(\frac{60-j}{60}\right)^{5} \cdot \cos\left(\frac{j}{30} \cdot \pi\right)\right]$$

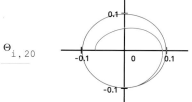

$\Theta_{i, 20}$

$\Pi_{i, 20}$

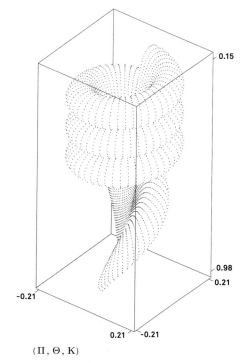

$(\Pi, \Theta, K)$

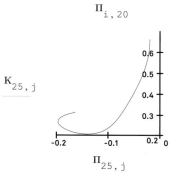

$K_{25, j}$

$\Pi_{25, j}$

Length: 28 mm | Diameter: 15 mm
Cooking Time: 8–9 min

# TUBETTI RIGATI

The smallest members of the *pasta corta* (short pasta) clan, *tubetti rigati* (grooved tubes) were first created in Campania, southern Italy. When served *e fagioli* (with beans) they create very filling soups, but can also be served in a light *marinara* (mariner's) sauce of tomato, basil and onions.

> BENT LONGITUDINAL PROFILE
>
> ⌄ HOLLOW CROSS-SECTION
>
> ⌄ STRIATED SURFACE
>
> ⌄ SMOOTH EDGES

_ranges

$i := 0, 1 .. 150$

$j := 0, 1 .. 30$

_equations

$$\Pi_{i,j} := 2 \cdot \cos\left(\frac{i}{75} \cdot \pi\right) + 0.03 \cdot \sin\left(\frac{4 \cdot i + 7.5}{15} \cdot \pi\right) + 0.5 \cdot \cos\left(\frac{j}{60} \cdot \pi\right)$$

$$\Theta_{i,j} := 2 \cdot \sin\left(\frac{i}{75} \cdot \pi\right) + 0.03 \cdot \sin\left(\frac{4 \cdot i}{15} \cdot \pi\right) + 0.5 \cdot \sin\left(\frac{j}{60} \cdot \pi\right)$$

$$K_{i,j} := \frac{j}{3}$$

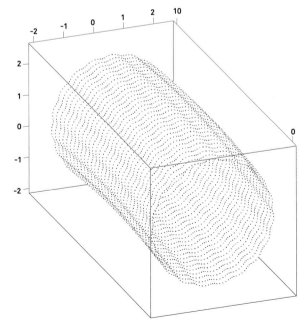

$(\Pi, \Theta, K)$

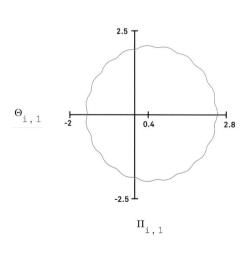

$\Theta_{i,1}$

$\Pi_{i,1}$

Length: **11 mm** | Diameter: **5 mm**
Cooking Time: **11 min**

# ZITI

A pasta reserved for banquets and special occasions, *ziti* ('grooms' or 'brides' in Italian dialect) originate from Sicily. Tradition has it that they should be broken by hand before being tossed into boiling water. After draining they can be served in tomato sauces with peppers or courgettes, topped with cheeses like Provolone.

> STRAIGHT LONGITUDINAL PROFILE
⌄ HOLLOW CROSS-SECTION
⌄ SMOOTH SURFACE
⌄ SMOOTH EDGES

_ranges

$i := 0, 1 .. \ 70$

$j := 0, 1 .. \ 70$

_equations

$$\Pi_{i,j} := 0.5 \cdot \cos\left(\frac{i}{35} \cdot \pi\right) + 0.2 \cdot \sin\left(\frac{j}{70} \cdot \pi\right)$$

$$\Theta_{i,j} := 0.5 \cdot \sin\left(\frac{i}{35} \cdot \pi\right) + 0.2 \cdot \sin\left(\frac{j}{70} \cdot \pi\right)$$

$$K_{i,j} := \frac{j}{14}$$

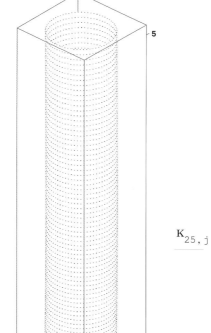

$(\Pi, \Theta, K)$

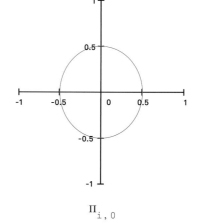

$\Theta_{i,0}$

$\Pi_{i,0}$

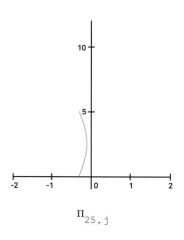

$K_{25,j}$

$\Pi_{25,j}$

Length: **255 mm** | Diameter: **7 mm**
Cooking Time: **7 min**

# THE FAMILY REUNION

## (Seating Plan)

_cross-section colour index:

Solid ◯
Hollow ◯
Semi-open ◯
Pasta with properties ◉
that mean it could sit
at either table

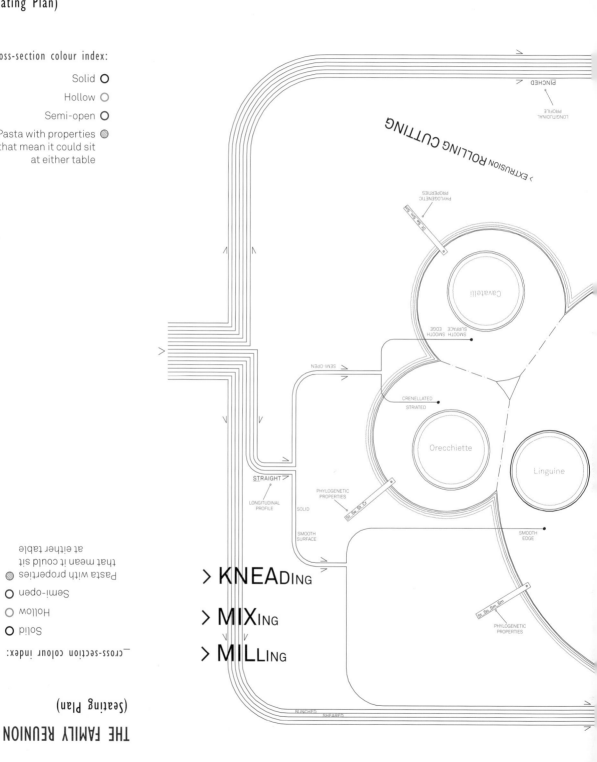

> EXTRUSION ROLLING CUTTING <

PINCHED
LONGITUDINAL
PROFILE

PHYLOGENETIC
PROPERTIES

Cavatelli

SMOOTH SMOOTH
SURFACE EDGE

SEMI-OPEN

CRENELLATED
STRIATED

Orecchiette

Linguine

STRAIGHT
LONGITUDINAL
PROFILE

SOLID

PHYLOGENETIC
PROPERTIES

SMOOTH
SURFACE

SMOOTH
EDGE

> KNEADing

> MIXing

> MILLing

BUNCHED
SHEARED

PHYLOGENETIC
PROPERTIES

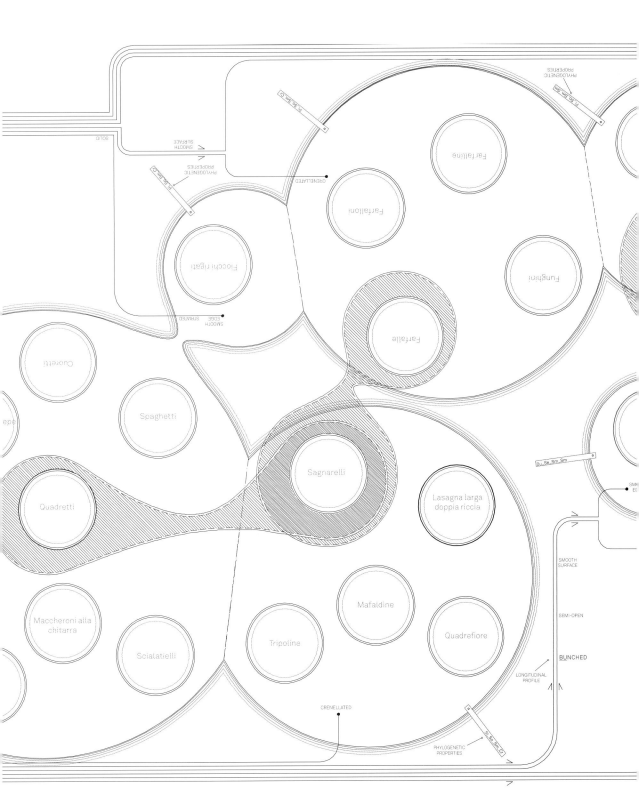

Farfalline

Farfalloni

Funghini

Flocchi rigati

Farfalle

Quoretti

Spaghetti

epe

Sagnarelli

Lasagna larga
doppia riccia

Quadretti

Maccheroni alla
chitarra

Mafaldine

Scialatielli

Tripoline

Quadrefiore

SOLID

SMOOTH
SURFACE

PHYLOGENETIC
PROPERTIES

PHYLOGENETIC
PROPERTIES

Fr_Se_Sm_Cr

Fr_Se_Sm_Sm

CRENELLATED

SMOOTH
EDGE

STRIATED

Bu_Se_Sm_Sm

SMOOTH
SURFACE

SEMI-OPEN

BUNCHED

LONGITUDINAL
PROFILE

SMC
EC

CRENELLATED

PHYLOGENETIC
PROPERTIES

St_Se_Sm_Cr

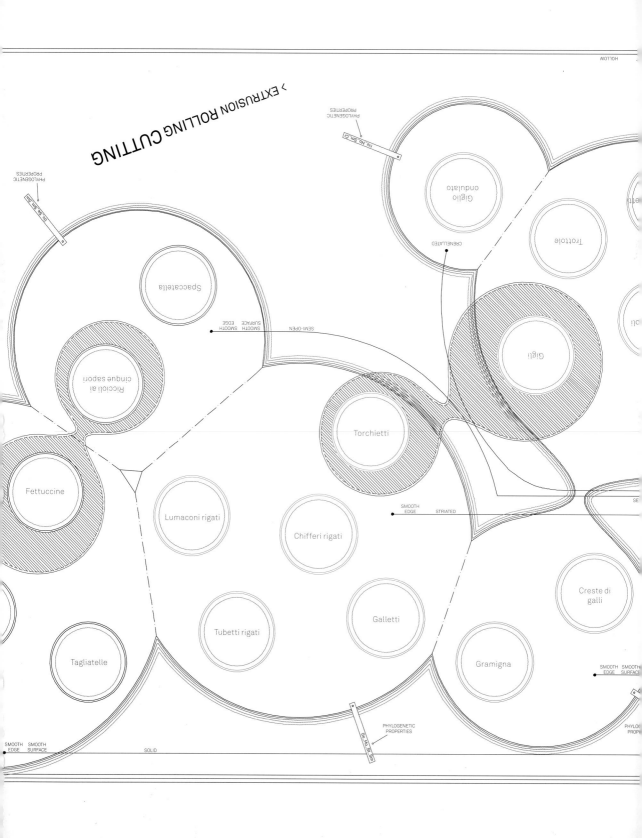

EXTRUSION ROLLING CUTTING

PHYLOGENETIC PROPERTIES

Be. Sc. Sm. Cy.

PHYLOGENETIC PROPERTIES

He. Ho. Sm. Cy.

HOLLOW

Spaccatella

Giglio ondulato

Trottole

CRENELLATED

Riccioli ai cinque sapori

SMOOTH   SMOOTH
EDGE   SURFACE   SEMI-OPEN

Giglí

Torchietti

Fettuccine

Lumaconi rigati

Chifferi rigati

SMOOTH
EDGE   STRIATED

SE

Creste di galli

Tagliatelle

Tubetti rigati

Galletti

Gramigna

SMOOTH   SMOOTH
EDGE   SURFACE

SMOOTH   SMOOTH
EDGE   SURFACE   SOLID

PHYLOGENETIC PROPERTIES

Be. Ho. Sc. Sm.

PHYLO
PROP

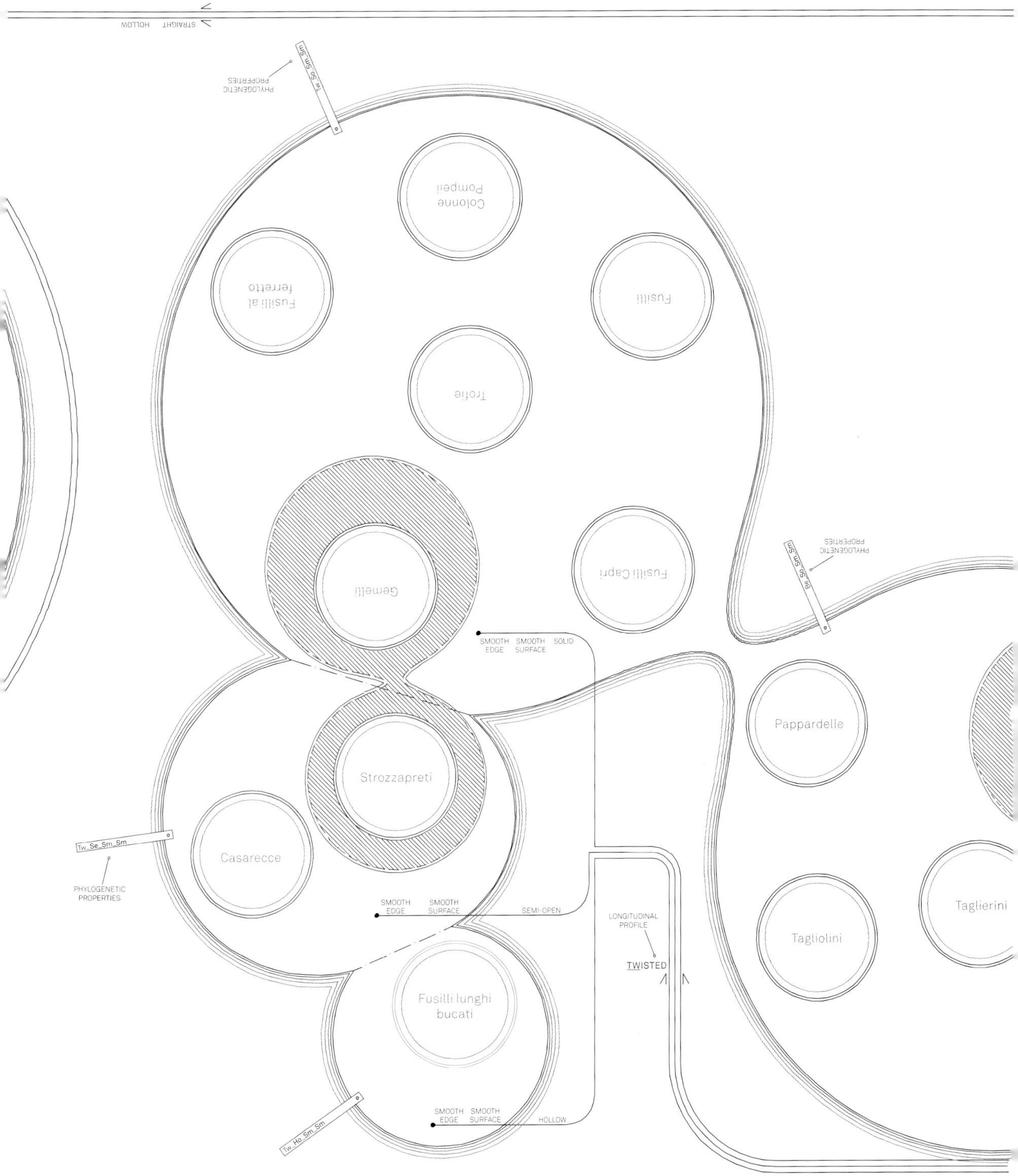

PHYLOGENETIC
PROPERTIES

Tw_Se_Sm_Sm

Colonne
Pompeii

Fusilli al
ferretto

Fusilli

Trofie

Gemelli

Fusilli Capri

PHYLOGENETIC
PROPERTIES

Se_Se_Sm_Sm

SMOOTH   SMOOTH   SOLID
EDGE      SURFACE

Strozzapreti

Pappardelle

Tw_Se_Sm_Sm

Casarecce

PHYLOGENETIC
PROPERTIES

SMOOTH        SMOOTH              SEMI-OPEN
EDGE           SURFACE

LONGITUDINAL
PROFILE

TWISTED

Taglierini

Tagliolini

Fusilli lunghi
bucati

Tw_Ho_Sm_Sm

SMOOTH   SMOOTH
EDGE      SURFACE          HOLLOW

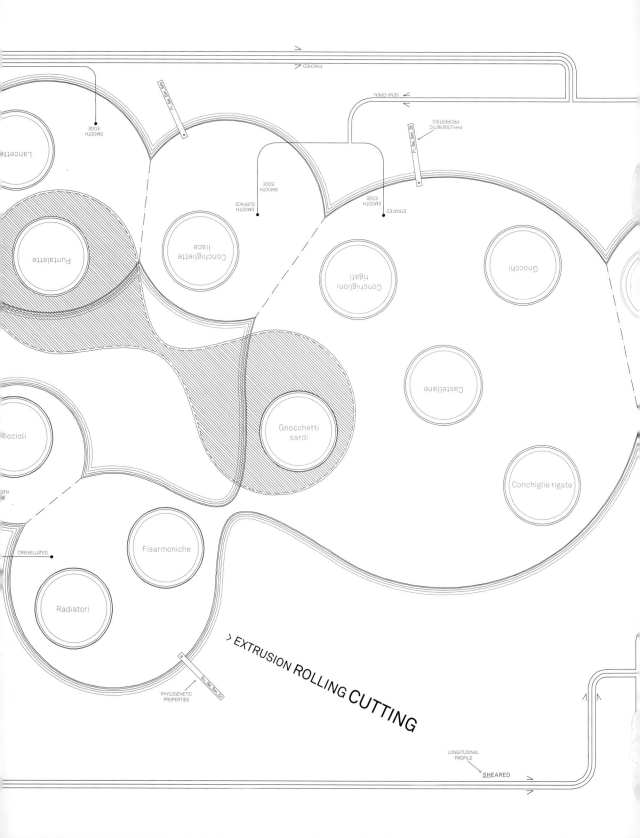

PINCHED

SEMI-OPEN

Pl Sa Sm St

SMOOTH
EDGE

Lancette

PHYLOGENETIC
PROPERTIES

Pl Sa Sm St

Puntalette

Conchigliette
lisce

SMOOTH
EDGE
SMOOTH
SURFACE

Conchiglioni
rigati

SMOOTH
EDGE
STRIATED

Gnocchi

Riccioli

Castellane

Gnocchetti
sardi

Conchiglie rigate

SMOOTH
E

CRENELLATED

Fisarmoniche

Radiatori

Pl Sa Sm Cr

PHYLOGENETIC
PROPERTIES

> EXTRUSION ROLLING CUTTING

LONGITUDINAL
PROFILE

SHEARED

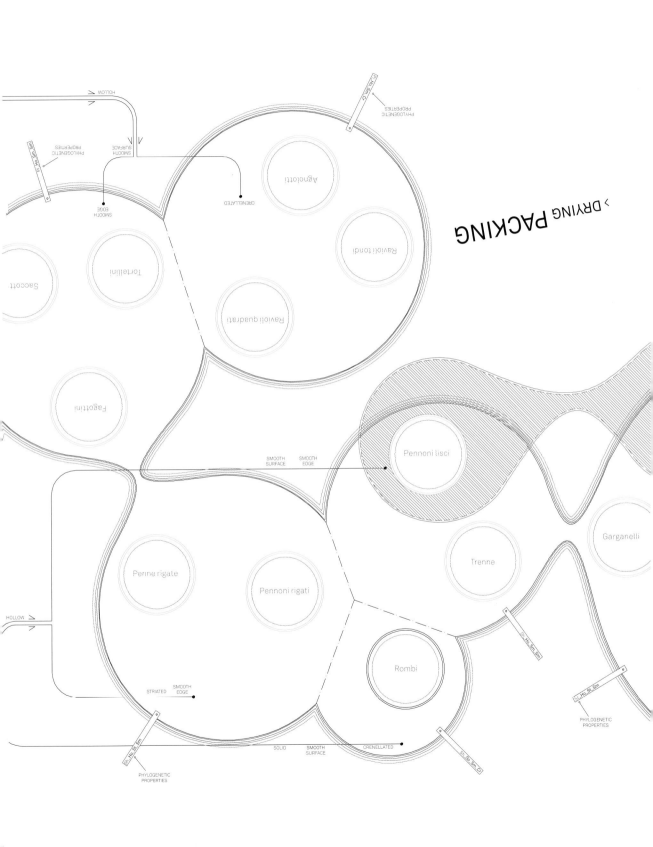

DRYING PACKING >

HOLLOW

PHYLOGENETIC
PROPERTIES

SMOOTH
SURFACE

St Ho Sm Sm

Agnolotti

PHYLOGENETIC
PROPERTIES

St Ho Sm Cr

SMOOTH
EDGE

CRENELLATED

Ravioli tondi

Saccoti

Tortellini

Ravioli quadrati

Fagottini

Pennoni lisci

SMOOTH
SURFACE

SMOOTH
EDGE

Trenne

Garganelli

St Ho Sm Sm

Penne rigate

Pennoni rigati

Rombi

HOLLOW

PHYLOGENETIC
PROPERTIES

St Ho St Sm

STRIATED

SMOOTH
EDGE

St Ho St Sm

PHYLOGENETIC
PROPERTIES

SOLID

SMOOTH
SURFACE

CRENELLATED

St Sn Sm Cr

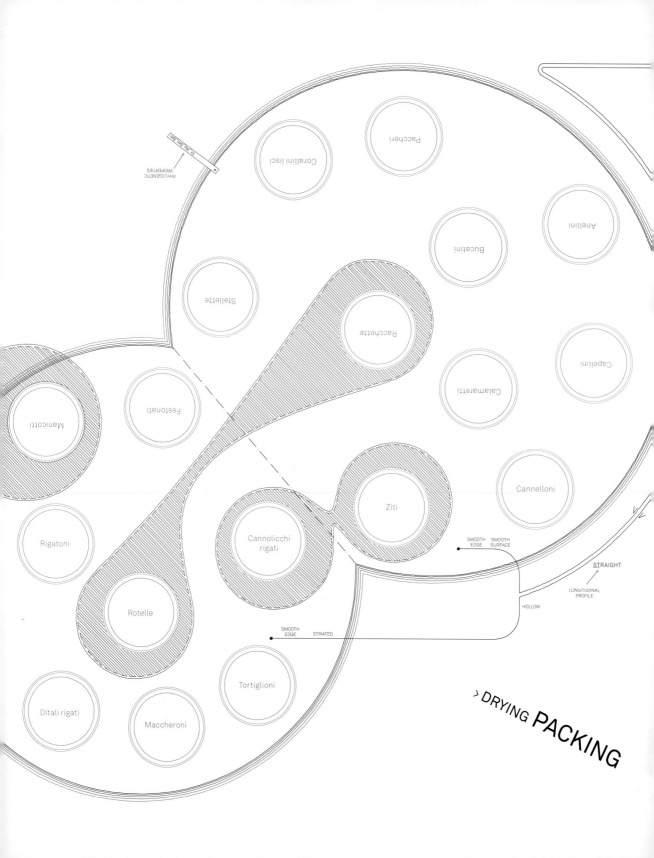

PHYLOGENETIC
PROPERTIES

Coralini lisci

Paccheri

Anellini

Bucatini

Stellette

Racchette

Capellini

Festonati

Calamaretti

Manicotti

Cannelloni

Rigatoni

Ziti

Cannolicchi rigati

SMOOTH SMOOTH
EDGE SURFACE

STRAIGHT

LONGITUDINAL
PROFILE

Rotelle

HOLLOW

SMOOTH
EDGE    STRIATED

Ditali rigati

Tortiglioni

Maccheroni

> DRYING PACKING

# THE FAMILY REUNION
(Seating Plan)

_cross-section colour index:

Solid ⃝
Hollow ⃝
Semi-open ⃝
Pasta with properties ◎
that mean it could sit
at either table

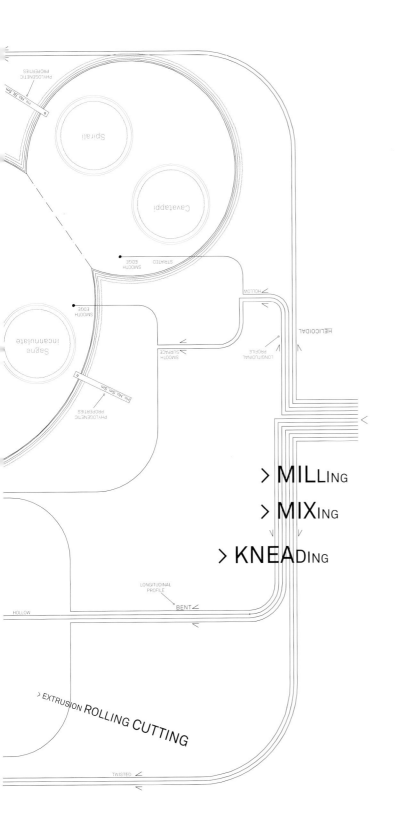

> MILLING
> MIXING
> KNEADING

EXTRUSION ROLLING CUTTING

at either table
that mean it could sit
Pasta with properties ◎
Semi-open ⃝
Hollow ⃝
Solid ⃝
_cross-section colour index:

(Seating Plan)
THE FAMILY REUNION

# INDEX OF COMMONLY KNOWN PASTA TYPES

This index lists all the commonly known pasta types, sorted according to **FAMILY**.

The varieties that appear in this book are coloured red and capitalized, and followed by the page number.

Other commonly known pasta types are sorted according to their properties. For example, *bavette* is indexed below SPAGHETTI, because they both share many of the same properties (straight profile, solid cross-section, smooth surface and smooth edges). Using this index and the diagrams in the book you should be able to locate old favourites, and hopefully find some new ones too.

**GNOCCHI**
GNOCCHETTI SARDI 096
Bastardui
Ciciones
Cutanei
Malloreddus
Mischiglio
Sorcetti
Spätzle
Streppa e caccialà
GNOCCHI 099
Canederli
Cassulli
Cojette
Donderet
Gnòc dè schelt
Gnocchi de ciadin
Gnudi
Kneidlach
Malfatti
Maneghi
Pasta reale

**PASTA CORTA**
BUCCOLI 022
CALAMARETTI 024
Fagioloni
Gasse
Maccheroni alla pecorara
CANNOLICCHI RIGATI 028
Canneroni
Stivaletti

CASARECCE 034
CASTELLANE 036
Pisarei
Scorze di mandorle
CAVATAPPI 039
Gobbetti
CAVATELLI 040
Cecatelli
Cuzzetielle
Rascatielli
CHIFFERI RIGATI 043
CONCHIGLIE RIGATE 046
Chinesini
DITALI RIGATI 058
Boccoletti
FARFALLE 063
FARFALLONI 066
FESTONATI 069
FIOCCHI RIGATI 072
FISARMONICHE 075
FUSILLI 079
Fischietti
Ghiottole
Rotini
GARGANELLI 088
Fusi istriani
GEMELLI 091
Cuzzi
Lorighitta
Passatelli
GIGLI 092

GIGLIO ONDULATO 094
Campanelle
GRAMIGNA 100
Bricchetti
MACCHERONI 110
Millerighe
Natalin
Sedani
MANICOTTI 117
ORECCHIETTE 118
Chiancaredde
Corzetti
Mescuetille
Pestazzule
Scorze di nocella
Sugeli
PACCHERI 121
PENNE RIGATE 124
Mostaccioli
PENNONI LISCI 127
PENNONI RIGATI 128
QUADREFIORE 132
RACCHETTE 136
RADIATORI 139
RICCIOLI 145
Rocchetti
RICCIOLI AI CINQUE
    SAPORI 146
Brodosini
Budelletti
Fojade

RIGATONI  148
ROMBI  150
Cresc'tajat
Fisckariedd'
Lenzolere e cuscenere
Maccheroni di ciaccio
Maltagliati
Paccozze
Patellette
Tacui
Zavardouni
ROTELLE  152
Ruote
SAGNARELLI  157
Abbotta pezziende
Blecs
Cenciono di fave
Fregnacce
Ladittas
Lunas
Pasta strappata
Schuncheneletz
SPACCATELLE  162
Ricciutelli
SPIRALI  167
Cellentani
STROZZAPRETI  172
Cazzaregli
TORCHIETTI  180
Trecce
TORTIGLIONI  185
Tufoli
TRENNE  187
TROFIE  190
Strigoli
TROTTOLE  192
TUBETTI RIGATI  194
Gargati

**PASTA LUNGA**
BUCATINI  021
Bigoli
Boccolotti
Maccheroni con lu ceppe
Perciatelli
Perciati
Shtridhelat
CAPELLINI  031
Barbina
Capellini d'angelo

Fidelini
Fili d'angelo
Filini
Maccheroncini di campofilone
Vermicelli
Zengarielle
COLONNE POMPEII  044
FETTUCCINE  070
Foglietti
Langanelle
Paglia e fieno
Pingiarelle
Suddhi
FUSILLI AL FERRETTO  081
Busa
Cajubi
Ferrazzuoli
Fileja
Mescuetille
Trucioli
FUSILLI CAPRI  082
FUSILLI LUNGHI BUCATI  084
LINGUINE  107
Strettine
Stroncatelli
Torcelli
MACCHERONI ALLA CHITARRA
     112
MAFALDINE  114
Ondine
Reginette toscane
Stracci
Tacconi
PAPPARDELLE  122
Battolli
Pappicci
Toppe
Strascinati umbri
SAGNE INCANNULATE  158
Busiata
SCIALATIELLI  160
Cecamariti
Ciriole
Code di topo
Pencarelli
Picchiettini
Pizzarelle
Sbrofadej
SPAGHETTI  165
Bavette

Bringoli
Cordelle calabresi
Cordelle sabine
Filati
Frigulozzi
Lombrichelli
Manate
Pici
Pinguni
Umbricelli
Vipere cieche
TAGLIATELLE  174
Alisanzas
Blutnudeln
Lagane
Picagge
Pizzoccheri
Tirache trevigiane
Trenette
TAGLIERINI  176
Fieno di canepina
Lunghetti
Matasse
Penchi
Stringozzi
Struncatura
TAGLIOLINI  179
Pillus
Schnalzernudeln
Sucamele
Tajarin
TRIPOLINE  188
ZITI  196
Candele
Mparrettati

**PASTA RIPIENA**
AGNOLOTTI  016
Agnoli di mostardele
Agnolini mantovani
Cadunsei
Caicc
Calcioni
Carlhù
Cjalsons
Coronette
Fioroni
Gattafin
Impanadas
Pannicelli
Pansotti

Panzerotto
Rufioi della valle dei mocheni
Scarfiuni
Schultzkrapfen
Turtei della valle tanaro
CANNELLONI  027
Rotolo ripieno
Schiaffettoni
Sigarette
Stracci di antrodoco
CAPPELLETTI  032
Cappellacci di zucca
Cappelletti dei briganti
Cappelletti umbri
Cappieddi 'i prieviti
Cappuccili
CONCHIGLIONI RIGATI  051
CRESTE DI GALLI  054
FAGOTTINI  060
Turtej cu la cua
GALLETTI  086
LASAGNA LARGA DOPPIA
    RICCIA  104
Filindeu
LUMACONI RIGATI  108
Gomiti
RAVIOLI QUADRATI  140
Barbagiuai
Calzonicchi
Fattisu
Graviuole molisane
Purulzoni
Raviore
Slicofi
Tordei

RAVIOLI TONDI  143
Anolini
Krafi
Marubini
Offelle
Ravioli alagnesi
Zembi d'arzillo
SACCOTTINI  155
Caramelle
Pi fasacc
Turtres ladine
TORTELLINI  182
Casonsei
Culingionis
Laianelle
Mandili 'nversoi
Scarpinocc

**PASTINE MINUTE**
ACINI DI PEPE  015
Cuscus
Fregula
Grattata
Pizzicotti
Scucuzun
Semola battuta
Tempesta
ANELLINI  018
Alfabeto
Occhi di passero
Occhi di pernice
CONCHIGLIETTE LISCE  048
CORALLINI LISCI  053
Diavolini
Gloria patri

Grandine
Paternoster
Pepe bucato
CUORETTI  057
FARFALLINE  064
FUNGHINI  076
Assabesi
Sorprese
LANCETTE  103
Tria
PUNTALETTE  130
Armellette
Biavetta
Cazzellitti
Frascarelli
Menietti
Mignaculis
Millefanti
Orzo
Pigné
Risone
Semi d'avena
QUADRETTI  135
Mariconda
Ptresenelle
Volarelle
Zizziridd'
STELLETTE  168
Avemarie
Lentine
STORTINI  171
Farfel
Menuzze

# ACKNOWLEDGMENTS

Many thanks to Thames & Hudson for supporting the project from its inception; Jean-Aimé Shu, a young French architect at IJP, for carrying the project forward; Stefano Graziani, for the exquisite photography lying at the heart of this book; Woonyin Mo Wong, for the illustration of the Pasta Family Reunion (seating plan); Niccolò Marini for his diligent layout work; Mrs Marini, for helping us get hold of rare Roman varieties during the preliminary phases; and Marco Guarnieri, for providing the inspiration, and for many enjoyable evenings of warmth, wine and *pastasciutta*.